MAXnotes®

Euripides'

Medea and Electra

Text by
Tamara L. Underiner
(Ph.C. University of Washington)
School of Drama
University of Washington
Seattle, Washington

Illustrations by
Thomas E. Cantillon

Research & Education Association

What **MAXnotes®** *Will Do for You*

This book is intended to help you absorb the essential contents and features of Euripides' *Medea* and *Electra* and to help you gain a thorough understanding of the work. The book has been designed to do this more quickly and effectively than any other study guide.

For best results, this **MAXnotes** book should be used as a companion to the actual work, not instead of it. The interaction between the two will greatly benefit you.

To help you in your studies, this book presents the most up-to-date interpretations of every section of the actual work, followed by questions and fully explained answers that will enable you to analyze the material critically. The questions also will help you to test your understanding of the work and will prepare you for discussions and exams.

Meaningful illustrations are included to further enhance your understanding and enjoyment of the literary work. The illustrations are designed to place you into the mood and spirit of the work's settings.

The **MAXnotes** also include summaries, character lists, explanations of plot, and episode-by-episode analyses. A biography of the author and discussion of the work's historical context will help you put this literary piece into the proper perspective of what is taking place.

The use of this study guide will save you the hours of preparation time that would ordinarily be required to arrive at a complete grasp of this work of literature. You will be well prepared for classroom discussions, homework, and exams. The guidelines that are included for writing papers and reports on various topics will prepare you for any added work which may be assigned.

The **MAXnotes** will take your grades "to the max."

Dr. Max Fogiel
Program Director

Contents

**Each episode includes List of Characters,
Summary, Analysis, Study Questions and
Answers, and Suggested Essay Topics.**

SECTION ONE

Introduction

The Life and Work of Euripides

Perhaps more than any of the other dramatists of the Greek classic age, Euripides appeals to modern audiences. Compared to the work of Aeschylus and Sophocles—the only other writers of tragedies whose work has survived the millenia—Euripides' plays treat the human side of the dilemmas they present in a way that still captures our imagination.

In his work, Euripides is not content to believe in the ultimate wisdom and goodness of the gods, and his heroes and heroines are not the almost superhuman figures that appear in other plays of the age. Like the other dramatists, Euripides drew his characters from the realm of myth and tales of epic heroism, but his protagonists are drawn on a more human scale. Some commentators go so far as to credit him with the birth of an early form of "psychological drama."

Euripides' characters often challenge divine wisdom, disrupt divine order, and face situations for which there are no easy answers in their attempts to make sense of their world. In this, they are rarely guided or opposed by the actual presence of divinities on stage, unlike the heroes and heroines of Aeschylus and Sophocles.

Although it is difficult to pinpoint exactly the circumstances of his birth, life and death, scholars have been able to piece together a rather rough outline. He was most probably born in 484 B.C., four years before Athens was victorious in the Persian Wars. The son of a merchant and a high–born woman, he grew to maturity in the time in which Athens reached its height as the center of democracy and culture in the ancient Greek world.

Among the thinkers who influenced Euripides' own intellectual develepment were Anaxagoras, Protagoras, Aeschylus, and his pupil, Socrates. Some of these philosophers came to be categorized as "Sophists," a term which originally meant "professional teachers" but later took on more derogatory connotations. It was associated with those who taught the skills necessary to win in public debates—skills which relied more on persuasive speaking abilities than on a commitment to the truth. (The reader might keep this in mind when considering the relative skills of Medea and her opponents in the debates which occur in *Medea*.)

But it was as a poet, not a philosopher, that Euripides has left his mark on subsequent generations. He entered his first dramatic competition in 455 B.C., and took his first top prize (for a play that has not survived) in 441 B.C. In those days, playwrighting competitions were a key part in festivals marking various religious occasions. His *Medea* was written in 431 B.C.; *Electra*, in approximately 412 B.C. In all, he composed 92 plays, only 19 of which survived intact.

Much of his work was well received, building his reputation not only in Athens, but in other cities in the Greek world. Five of his plays took top prizes; several more took second in the final rounds of the dramatic competitions. Others fared less well, perhaps because they challenged contemporary notions of religious tradition, social mores, and the content of the legends from which he drew his material. Such legends were sacred to Athens, proving the divine sanction of her status as leader of the Greek empire. To change or question them would have seemed an act approaching heresy and treason, though Euripides was not the loudest of the voices against tradition in his time.

Much of his work was completed during the Pelopponesian wars that eventually destroyed Athens; in repsonse, some of his plays are overtly patriotic, while others are just as critical of Athens' role in those wars. Sometime after 408 B.C., Euripides left Athens for Macedonia, where he composed perhaps his greatest work, *The Bacchae*. He died there two years later. According to legend, he spent his final days in solitude, living in caves overlooking the sea.

Despite a long history of scholarly debates over the merits of Euripides' work, the fact remains that none of the other playwrights of the period has been more often produced or quoted in the centuries that have followed. Some scholars have dismissed his work for being too "easy," for lacking artistic unity, or for dwelling too often on the sordid side of life. Many others have praised it for its innovative and experimental qualities, and its honest approach to difficult and sometimes impossible situations. Yet Euripides' commitment to exploring both sides of the dramatic debates he stages, and his deep interest in the underlying psychological and emotional bases for human motivation, have created dramas that continue to haunt our imagination more than 2000 years later.

Historical Background

The achievements of Greece in its classic period have been considered unparalleled in the history of Western civilization. In 511 B.C., a political leader named Cleisthenes overthrew Athens' last tyrant and instituted a radical form of government called democracy. Against a background of almost constant turmoil—first, the victorious struggle against Persian invaders that ended with the battle of Salamis in 480 B.C., then later the unsuccessful Peloponnesian wars against Sparta—Athens built, and then lost, an empire. During this time, her politicians, philosophers and poets all debated the great questions of the age: the meaning of life and death; the role of religion, tradition, and ethics; and the relative influence on human activity of nature versus customs, laws, social conventions and practices. What emerged throughout this century of struggle was a fierce commitment to individual freedom, tempered by social responsibility and moderated by laws established in this, the world's first and most extensive democracy.

This achievement alone has secured for Athens a singular place in the history of the West. In Athens, the rights the new democracy conferred did not extend to all members of Athenian society—only to free men. Women and slaves fared less well, and it is important to keep this in mind while reading plays like *Medea* and *Electra*, both of which feature strong-willed women whose actions and temperments are different from what was prescribed for the women of the time.

In fifth–century Athens, women, like slaves, were little more than the property of men, with no legal rights to citizenship, the vote, education, property ownership, or self–representation in the courts of law. In 451 B.C., when Pericles passed new laws limiting citizenship to those born of sons of Athenian free men, married to daughters of the same, such Athenian daughters became the most sought–after "goods" in the city.

It is interesting to note that in the Greek language there was no word for "woman" as we know it; their word *gynos*, translates literally as "under the yoke," and was used to mean "wife." In classical Greece, women were referred to almost exclusively in terms of their relationship to a man. Respectable women kept to themselves, lived in separate quarters away from their husbands, and prepared but did not share in their meals. A group of women, called *hetairai*, did enjoy more freedoms. Courtesans or "kept women," the *hetairai* had access to education and could accompany men in public; but their offspring could never become Athenian citizens.

As the roles and aims of women have changed over time, so has Euripides' reputation among women and men. In his own day, he was labeled a misogynist by many, because many of his characters, Medea and Electra among them, behaved in ways that would have scandalized the respectable Athenian citizenry. Later, one of Medea's own speeches was taken up by early suffragists, as an eloquent way to express the ongoing plight of women in male–dominated societies of the nineteenth and twentieth centuries.

Drama in Ancient Greece

Ancient Greeks came to a day at the theatre with something approaching religious awe. Plays were staged at the great festivals held in honor of Dionysus, and every citizen was expected to attend. They were held in large amphitheatres carved into the hillsides and fitted with stone seats, that could hold more than 15,000 people.

Several festivals were held each year in Athens and the surrounding area; the winners in playwrighting competitions went on to compete in the Great Dionysia festival, held yearly in Athens. Men played all the acting roles, which were shared among no more than three actors. There is some debate about whether women sometimes danced in the choruses.

In the competitions, three poets were selected to submit four plays each (three tragedies and one comic "satyr" play). All four from each playwright would be staged on each of three performance days. At the end of the festival a panel of five judges would award first, second and third prizes. Between 455 and 408 B.C., Euripides took the top prize eight times.

From the hundreds and hundreds of plays written during this period (more than a thousand of which made it to the Great Dionysia), only 33 have survived. From the work of Aeschylus we have only seven, from Sophocles also seven, and from Euripides 19; all but two of which are tragedies.

By far, the majority of these plays treated subjects that were already well known to their audiences as myths drawn from the Homeric oral storytelling tradition. The appeal was to see how the playwright would select and construct the incidents from a long epic, into a tightly structured hour or so of drama. This selection and arrangement of incidents Aristotle called "plot," and he gave it primary importance over the other elements of drama: "thought" (theme), character, "diction" (dialogue), music, and spectacle.

Most Greek tragedies follow a similar pattern. They open with a prologue—spoken by a character, a chorus member, or a god— which provide necessary background leading up to the events in the play. Then comes the *parados,* or first entrance of the chorus, singing and dancing. "Chorus," as understood in the Greek sense, was comprised of citizens of the city in which the play's action occurred. The Greek chorus served several functions: to comment on the action of the play; give advice to the main characters; establish the overall social or ethical framework from which the actions of the main characters can be judged; set the overall tone or mood of the play and theatrical elements.

Following the *parados* is a series of three to six episodes in which the action of the play proceeds. These episodes are punctuated by choral odes and choral passages called *stasima.* Plays usually conclude with an *exodos,* the final choral song and dance.

Greek tragedy usually begins as we see the consequences of earlier decisions made by humans or gods as they lead to a point of crisis in the play. As a result, the action of the plays typically takes place in a single day. Often, the crisis is caused by some human frailty on the part of the main character, referred to as *hamartia* and often translated as the "tragic flaw."

According to Aristotle, the best of the tragedies feature a change in fortune, from good to bad, of an essentially good man. The reversal (called *peripeteia*) is usually marked by a key scene of recognition, or *anagnorisis*, in which the main character reaches the point of no return as he or she commits to following the dictates of fate.

It is a commonplace definition of tragedy as "a play where the hero dies," but a review of Greek tragedies reveals that such is not always the case. Just as often, the hero or heroine's fate is to be exiled from his or her homeland; in the culture of the ancient Greeks, this may have been a fate tantamount to, or worse than, death itself.

The result of watching the character play out his or her destiny is to achieve what Aristotle called *catharsis*, the release or purging of emotions through the experience of pity and fear: pity for the unmerited misfortunes of the hero or heroine; and fear that such a thing could befall any human being. The outcome of this *catharsis*, according to Aristotle, is not to leave the spectators in a state of dangerous agitation; rather, it is to create in them a heightened state of awareness that would carry over into their everyday lives.

Mythological Background to Medea

Audiences attending the first performance of *Medea* in 431 B.C. would have already been familiar with numerous versions of the story that went back to the time of the *Odyssey*. Though these events are recapped at various points in the play, it is helpful to keep them in mind before starting it, in order to better approximate its impact on the play's original audience.

Medea was a native of the distant land of Colchis, far away from Athens on the east coast of the Black Sea. Her father was the sorcerer and king, Aietes, son of the sun god Helios (or Phoebus) and keeper of the Golden Fleece. Jason and his crew of the Argo had sailed to Colchis, where they had been sent by his uncle Pelias in search of the Golden Fleece. Medea met and fell deeply in love with Jason, eventually using her own powers of sorcery to help him avoid the traps set between him and the Golden Fleece–this included murdering and dismembering her own brother to distract the Colchians while Jason made his escape, taking Medea and the fleece with him.

The pair then settled in Jason's homeland of Iolcos, where Pelias cheated him of his claim to the throne. Once again Medea came to Jason's rescue, tricking the king's daughters into murdering their own father. But instead of ascending to the throne, Jason and Medea once more had to make an escape, going from Iolcos to Corinth with their two children. It is in Corinth where the action of the play takes place.

Jason decided to make a politically expedient marriage to the daughter of the Corinthian king, Creon, so that he could establish a new, royal bloodline. His plans were foiled conclusively by Medea, who used her powers to murder both the bride and her father. She in turn made her escape to Athens, where she subsequently married her protector, King Aegeus, who would become known as the father of the great Greek hero, Theseus.

In Euripides' dramatic treatment of the myth, Medea kills her own children by Jason in order to ensure that he will have no heirs. It is interesting to note that in no other earlier version of the story was this the case. In one account, Jason abandoned Medea, not because he wanted to remarry, but because she had concealed the children in the sanctuary of the goddess Hera, hoping to make them immortal. In other versions, the children were murdered by the Corinthian women or by Creon's henchmen—either in revenge for her murder of him and his daughter, or out of resentment toward being ruled by a non–Greek "barbarian."

Although none of the several other versions of the myth relates Medea's act of infanticide, Euripides' invention has taken hold most tenaciously, adding fuel to the debates over the playwright's alleged misogyny. Certainly it shocked the original audience, who would have been disturbed by the license he took with the myth.

Master List of Characters

Tutor—*Servant of Medea, minder of her two children.*

Nurse—*Servant of Medea.*

Chorus—*Corinthian women.*

Medea—*Native of Colchis, granddaughter of the sun god, wife of Jason; regarded as a sort of sorceress.*

Creon—*King of Corinth, Jason's new father–in–law.*

Jason—*Leader of the Argonauts, now in exile in Corinth, where he is about to marry the daughter of Creon.*

Aegeus—*King of Athens.*

Messenger—*One of Jason's servants.*

Two children—*Medea's and Jason's young boys.*

Summary of the Play

After having successfully stolen the Golden Fleece, Jason has been living in exile in Corinth with Medea and their children. On the day of the play's action, Jason abandons Medea, who is a native of Colchis and is considered to be a barbarian, to marry the daughter of the king of Corinth. Jason argues that by so doing he will be able to establish a legitimate line of heirs.

Because Medea's reputation as a sorceress has preceded her, she is viewed as a threat to Corinth if she remains there. Creon, the Corinthian king and Jason's new father–in–law, decides to protect himself and his family by banishing Medea from the kingdom. Gaining the sympathy of the Corinthian women, Medea begs for, and receives, one more day to get her affairs in order. She uses this time to plot her revenge against Jason and Creon.

First, she secures the promise of safe harbor from Aegeus, the king of Athens, in return for curing him of his impotence. Then she sends her children to the princess, bearing a wedding gift of a robe and crown she has poisoned, so that the wearer and anyone who touches its wearer will die a horrible death. The gift is accepted and the princess is killed. In trying to save her, her father Creon is also destroyed. Finally, Medea wreaks her most terrible act of vengeance. After much soul searching, she murders her own children by the sword, thus effectively cutting off Jason's present and future bloodlines.

When Jason returns from the palace, after having lost his bride, the Chorus informs him of Medea's other deed. He vows to kill her, but she is already out of reach in a chariot bound for Athens. In despair, he begs her to let him bury the children's bodies, a request she denies him. Instead, she bears them off with her, to bury them in a place where none of her enemies can desecrate their graves— leaving Jason and the Chorus to mourn before the gods, who may or may not hear their call.

Estimated Reading Time

Reading time will vary slightly according to the translation being used. Some modern translations are written in a very accessible style, while older verse translations are written in a more lofty style that takes more time to read. In general, allow two to three hours for a close reading of the entire work.

For full effect, *Medea* reads best in a single sitting. You may wish to break it up into two sessions, however. If so, the best division is through the end of the Choral section following Aegeus' exit. At this point, Medea's plans have been laid, and the second half will describe how she carries them out.

Medea

Prologue and Parados

New Characters:

Nurse: *loyal servant of Medea*

Tutor: *servant of Medea and minder of her children, friendly with Nurse*

The Children: *Medea's two young boys*

Medea: *(offstage only) native of Colchis, wife of Jason, a type of sorceress*

Chorus: *Corinthian women, friendly to Medea*

Summary

Medea's Nurse opens the play, lamenting the events that have brought Medea's household to its current state of crisis. If Jason had not sailed with the Argonauts to Colchis, Medea would never have met him and brought them all to Corinth. All has been relatively peaceful of late, but now, with Jason's decision to marry the king's daughter, Medea loses all her rights and is ill with hatred and grief—grief for the dissolution of her current family, and for her own betrayal of her former family. The nurse fears that Medea is plotting something terrible, as she is a "woman to fear."

There follows perhaps the only humourous moment in the play, as the children enter with their tutor, who has news from the

palace which the Nurse tries to coax out of him. Eventually we learn from the Tutor of King Creon's plans to banish Medea from his kingdom. Meanwhile, Medea is heard wailing her grief offstage.

The Nurse, knowing how her mistress gets when she's angry, is fearful for the safety of the children and begs the Tutor to keep them away from her. She then indulges in a brief monologue in which she extolls the advantages of ordinary life, removed from the grand passions that rule her royal masters and exact high retribution from the gods.

As Medea continues her offstage lament, the Chorus of Corinthian women enters, asking the Nurse for an explanation. Medea recounts some of the sacrifices she made on Jason's behalf, and longs for death. The Chorus is quick to reassure her that Jason is not worth that price, and begs the Nurse to bring Medea out so they can console her. With misgivings, the Nurse goes into the palace, leaving the Chorus to express their sympathy for a woman wronged by her husband's failure of faith.

Analysis

This prologue and *parados* do more than sketch in some of the necessary background to the story of Medea and Jason, which the audience would already have known anyway. Rather, it sets out some of the key motifs that will run through the play, and provides some foreshadowing of the characters and events which will dominate it.

The Nurse and Tutor, though relatively minor characters, become the voice of "ordinary" mortals. As the Nurse recounts the peaceful time in Corinth, we see the way Medea has tried to live as such a mortal, doing

> ...good service to the citizens
> Of her new country, and she fitted in
> As well with Jason's every wish. For women,
> That's the best way to make yourself secure:
> Never stand up and argue with a man. (15)

Later, she speaks in praise of moderation, a key theme circulating among the Greeks of the time, when she gives thanks for being born low, so as not to have to live in the extremes of passion as her masters do:

> For man should live with limit and measure;
> That is a phrase we often use,
> And it's proved true: Going beyond,
> Going too far, brings no advantage.
> It only means, when the gods are angry,
> They extract a greater price. (19)

The Tutor, too, is a refreshing example of everyday humanity that will stand in sharp contrast to the speech and behavior of his masters. He affectionately refers to the Nurse as an old "heirloom," and admits to having gotten his information by lurking around the palace eavesdropping on old men playing board games. Together with the Chorus, the Nurse and Tutor serve as a sort of stand–in for the audience, commenting on what they see, from the perspective of more reasonable men and women.

From the Nurse and the Chorus, as well as from Medea's words before we meet her in person, we learn a great deal about the kind of woman she is. Time and time again the Nurse expresses her fear over what Medea will do in her anger, afraid that she will turn on her friends as well as her foes in the blindness of her rage. Remembering that Medea's eventual infanticide was a Euripidean invention, we can speculate about the effect of the Nurse's several mentions of her fear for the children's safety. Perhaps the original audience would have assumed the Nurse was a dithering old slave who was over–dramatizing things.

Consider some of the imagery invoked by the Nurse in her descriptions of her mistress. She refers to her as a "beast about to charge."(17) In her "savage mood"(18) she is "wild with hate."(18) She is "like a savage beast with new–born young."(21) The Nurse wonders what her "untameable spirit [will] do under the bite of suffering."(18) Some critics have suggested that this imagery of savagery and bestiality got double mileage, not only to represent the desperation of a woman wronged, but also to mark the characteristics of Medea as a non–Greek "barbarian" to Greek audiences. This would serve to displace the fear of Medea's reactions on to an "other," who would not be expected to act like a civilized Greek. Thus, the spectacle of Medea's revenge could play itself out to an audience who could reassure themselves that "such things could never happen to us."

The Chorus, too, is concerned about Medea, but more so for her own welfare. Remember, they don't know her as well as the Nurse does, and they have been living with the Medea who has tried to act like any good Greek woman would. All they want is to console her, and it is clear from their closing ode that they view Jason as the evil one, who broke a sacred promise by his ill treatment of his wife.

What of Medea in the opening moments of the play? Her off-stage wailing is filled with despair, grief, anger, and all the "fury of a woman scorned." From her own mouth we hear the threat facing her children:

> ...O cursed children
> Of an unloved mother, may you die!
> Die with your father! May the whole
> Family of Jason perish!

No one on stage, and perhaps in the audience, is quite ready to believe this threat. Medea's subsequent speeches are filled more with grief and remorse than with fury. She is a complex creature, presented to us first as a woman driven to the limits of her sanity. And thus is set the stage for Euripides' great drama.

Study Questions

1. Where does the action of the prologue and *parados* take place?

2. What is Medea's homeland?

3. List three crimes Medea has committed on Jason's behalf.

4. How long have Medea and her family been exiled in Corinth?

5. What has Jason done to cause Medea such pain?

6. Who is to be banished by Creon's orders?

7. What does the Nurse think Jason will do about the banishment?

8. Why do the Nurse, Tutor, Chorus and Medea herself think

Jason has left her?

9. Where is Medea during the opening moments of the play?

10. What is the Chorus's reaction to Medea's grief?

Answers

1. The action takes place outside a palace near Corinth.

2. Medea is a native of Colchis.

3. She betrayed her father, killed her brother, and tricked the daughters of King Pelias into killing their father.

4. Medea and her family have been living in Corinth a matter of some years: the Chorus refers to having known her over the years, but her children are still young.

5. Jason has decided to marry the daughter of the king of Corinth, thus abandoning Medea to the status of a woman with no male protection or rights.

6. Medea and her children are to be banished, according to the rumors of Creon's orders.

7. The Nurse believes Jason will never consent to his children being banished. This later proves untrue.

8. The characters all seem to believe that Jason has tired of Medea, and is looking for a "change of bed."

9. Medea has locked herself in her rooms at her palace.

10. The Chorus sympathizes with Medea against Jason, and wants to comfort her before she hurts herself or others.

Suggested Essay Topics

1. Given the information provided so far through the words of the characters and Chorus, what is the picture being painted of Medea? What might we expect of her in the course of the play, given the hints dropped by the Nurse, who knows her well, and the Chorus, who knows her less well? Provide support for your opinions with excerpts from the play.

2. What kind of tone, or mood, does Euripides set in these

opening moments, and what leads you to that conclusion? What stylistic devices does he employ to do so? Examples might be the use of imagery, comic relief, calls upon the gods, the interruptions of Medea's off–stage cries, etc.

Medea
First Episode: Medea and Creon

New Character:

Creon: *King of Corinth, father of Medea's rival*

Summary

Medea emerges from her palace to address the Corinthian women gathered outside. In a long speech, she appeals to their gender to understand her plight, by enumerating the inequities women face in their relationships with men. Her situation is further complicated by her foreign status, which has left her without family to turn to in her despair. The speech closes with an appeal to the women to remain silent about any plans she makes to take her revenge on her faithless husband. The Chorus women express their sympathy, and pledge to say nothing.

Creon enters and immediately begins to insult Medea, calling her a "sour–faced woman, squalling at [her] husband." He proceeds to pronounce his banishment of her and the children, effective immediately. In blunt terms, he justifies this act by saying he is afraid of what she might do to his daughter, based on his knowledge of Medea's cleverness, her past history, and the threats she has made against his family. He hopes that by removing her from Corinth, she will no longer pose a threat to them.

Medea responds with bitter self–recrimination, lamenting the fact that her reputation is working against her, when in fact she considers herself to be "not that clever." She appeals to Creon, saying she does not hold this turn of events against him or his daughter, but against her husband, and promises to "keep the peace." Creon remains suspicious, however, and repeats his order.

What follows is an example of *stychomythia*, a series of rapid–fire exchanges between Medea and Creon, while they argue about whether she will stay or go. It ends with Medea pleading for "just one day" in order for her to get her affairs in order, and devise a plan for where she and her children will go. In this, she appeals to Creon's kindness as a father himself, claiming that it is not for her sake, but the children's, that she is asking. Creon relents, even though he still fears it is a mistake, and warns her that if she is still there after tomorrow, she will die.

After Creon exits, the Chorus once more expresses its empathy for Medea, and wonders what country will welcome her now. Medea replies by reminding them that it's not yet over. She "crawled and fawned" on Creon only to gain time to put other plans in motion, plans that despite her promises, harbour ill intent toward Creon and his daughter.

Medea then turns inward, debating with herself which course of action would be the most effective. Above all, she wishes her revenge to be definitive and final. There is to be no opportunity for her enemies to laugh at her when she's done. She decides to wait a little while, to see if an opportunity arises when she can claim her revenge and escape to a safe place of exile. Meanwhile, she swears by the gods that she will use every means at her disposal to achieve her ends, bitterly referring to those means as the womanly "arts of cowardice."

The Chorus closes this scene with a meditation on the cosmic ramifications of Medea's plight and its consequences. Jason's act has been shameful in the extreme, and reflects on all of Greece. Now all nature is turned upside down, and perhaps soon women "will have both rights and honour."

Analysis

From the moment Medea takes the stage, Euripides begins to flesh out her character beyond that of the legends about her, with which his original audiences would have been familiar. It is as a woman, not a witch, that Medea is able to strike a common chord with the Chorus of Corinthian women. And it is as a parent, not an unruly foreigner, that she is able to do the same with Creon. Nevertheless, we have the sense that behind these appeals to common humanity there is conscious calculation. There is a sense that Medea is indeed more clever than she claims, quite capable of using words to manipulate the emotions of her various audiences.

At the same time, as a woman alone in a foreign country, she cannot entirely succeed on her own—even with her reputed powers. It is imperative that she continue to cultivate the sympathy of the women, so that her enemies will not be alerted to her plans. Her first task, then, is to convince them that there is not so much difference between her and them. Their common lot as women puts them all in a position to potentially face what she herself is facing:

> Of all the creatures that have life and reason,
> We women are the most unhappy kind:
> First we must throw our money to the wind
> To buy a husband; and what's worse, we have to
> Accept him as the master of our body.
> Then comes the question that decides our lives:
> Is the master good or bad? (22)

Not surprisingly, it is the speech from which this is drawn that became a banner for feminists in the nineteenth and twentieth centuries, and taken out of context it is certainly an eloquent appeal. But it's important to keep in mind that Medea is not really an "ordinary" woman. She is the granddaughter of the sun god. She has been educated as Greek women wouldn't have been. She has further been trained in the use of powerful poisons, which has contributed to her reputation as a sorceress.

As a result, Medea is far less a victim of the strict rules applying to Greek women than is her audience of Corinthian women. While she makes valid points about the inequitable lot of women, her aim is not so much to argue against this situation as to ensure that, because she seems to share it, the Chorus will give her their cooperation.

Some recent critics have suggested that given the play's unthinkable ending, Euripides gave Medea this speech, and others, to alert Athenians to the dangers of allowing women to have too much power, as well as to turn sentiment against foreigners trying to establish lives in that city at the time. While this argument may have merit, it seems insufficient considering Euripides' treatment of Jason as well, which we will come to presently.

Within the drama itself, Medea's speech is surely taken at its face value by the Chorus. Imagine an inspired political speech in which the speaker "plays" the audience to a fevered emotional pitch, and you have some idea of Medea's effect in hers. One critic suggests that by the time she's finished, the Corinthian women have claimed Medea's vengeance as their own.

When Creon enters with his orders of banishment, we see a different side of Medea, one that is no less calculated to further her aims. Despite her claims to the contrary, this speech shows how truly clever, how quick Medea can be to "think on her feet". Up to now, Medea's agony has been due to Jason's treatment of her. Only now does she learn that her humiliation is to be compounded by banishment. After only a few lines to allow this to sink in, Medea quickly adopts a new strategy of appeasement, blatantly lying to Creon with her assurances that her hatred is targeted to Jason alone. She concedes defeat to the "stronger" Creon, and begs to be allowed to stay. When this is again denied her, she successfully negotiates for one more day, by drawing a connection between Creon's parental sentiments and her own.

In this appeal on behalf of her children, we see also an example of the playwright's skill in carrying the theme of the children forward through the action. At this point, the original audience would still be unaware of their eventual fate; but it could hardly fail to have been reminded of them and their central role in the drama, as it will unfold.

Medea's skills in the arts of persuasion are brought out in her next address to the Chorus, which shows how she has artfully manipulated Creon. In no uncertain terms, she vows to "turn three enemies to corpses—/The father and the daughter, and my husband." By the play's end, there will be four corpses, not three, and Jason's will not be among them. Through her craftiness, Medea has maneuvered herself into a position where the death by poison of her enemies is now possible, thanks to the way she "crawled and fawned on" the man who could have held her destiny more firmly in his grasp.

The scene ends with a further tribute to Medea's rhetorical skill. Convinced of the utter rightness of Medea's claims, the Chorus is moved to see them not as the result of one woman's misfortunes, but as a sign that the whole of nature has been turned on its head. Certainly, as we shall see, Corinth itself will be shaken to its roots by the ultimate consequences of Jason's choice. Perhaps for now, Medea's situation acts as a sort of trigger for them to express their own dissatisfaction with their lot. But the Chorus doesn't linger over this. Instead, they bring us back to the action of the play by once more rehearsing the list of Medea's grievances, and confirming their sympathy in them. As if summoned by their criticism, Jason then enters to face his formidable wife.

Study Questions

1. Why does Medea say she fears the Chorus will reproach her?

2. What does Medea say she'd rather do than "once give birth?"

3. What is her point in so saying?

4. Give three reasons why Creon fears Medea.

5. In what ways does Medea claim that having a reputation for being clever is in fact a liability to her?

6. What is Creon's initial response to Medea's claim that she harbors no ill will toward him and his family?

7. Give two reasons for Creon's granting Medea her wish to remain in Corinth for one more day.

8. In her speech following Creon's exit, who does Medea target for her revenge?

9. Why does Medea not act immediately upon this desire?

10. Why does the Chorus say, at the end of the episode, that there have been no women poets?

Answers

1. Having withdrawn into her rooms, Medea fears the Chorus will interpret this as a sign of arrogance and pride, of not desiring to fit in with the community.

2. Medea claims she would rather fight three times in battle than give birth once.

3. She says this to counter the claim that women lead risk–free lives within the safety of their homes.

4. Creon fears Medea because she is clever and has been part of evil happenings; she has been wounded by Jason's treatment of her; and she threatens to do harm to Creon's household.

5. Medea says clever people are envied and despised by others. "Stupid" people tend to think the clever are equally stupid, and those who consider themselves to be clever resent someone who is more clever.

6. Creon believes Medea's quiet assurances mask a more sinister reality, and he doesn't trust them.

7. Creon allows Medea to stay because he does not wish to appear to be a tyrant in his treatment of Medea. He also believes that one day is not long enough for Medea to do any harm.

8. Medea wishes "to turn three enemies to corpses"—Creon, his daughter, and Jason.

9. Medea decides to postpone her actions a little while, hoping that she'll be able to secure safe refuge after the deed is done. If not, she will risk her own death to ensure theirs.

10. The Chorus says there have been no women poets because Apollo, the god of song, never passed on his gifts to a member of their gender.

Suggested Essay Topics

1. Analyze the structure of Medea's first speech to the Chorus. How does she arrange her arguments for maximum effect?

2. Contrast the Medea of the opening speech to the Chorus with the one she presents to Creon. Does the tone she takes with each of them differ? If so, how, and to what effect? What are some of the strategies she uses to persuade them to her view? Are there any similarities worth noting between the two?

Medea
Second Episode: Medea and Jason

New Character:

Jason: *husband of Medea, about to marry Creon's daughter*

Summary

Jason enters, blaming Medea for her own misfortunes. It was one thing to complain against him, but by railing against the royal house she invited her banishment. This situation is nothing new. Jason claims he has often had to make amends for Medea's having displeased their hosts. Now it's too late, and Jason wants only to provide material help to Medea and the children before they go.

Medea responds angrily with a list of all the things she'd done, either out of love for Jason or at his direct request. She addresses the dangers she faced, the sacrifices she made, and the crimes she committed. To face a future in exile, with no prospect of welcome from even her old home, seems a bitter reward.

Point by point, Jason refutes her arguments. He claims his success was due to Aphrodite's intervention, not Medea's; and that Medea has since been privileged to live, famous, among the Greeks, rather than unknown among her fellow barbarians. His marriage to the Corinthian princess is simply part of a well-conceived plan that would have allowed them all to live in peace and prosperity together—if only Medea had held her tongue.

Here the longer monologues give way to a dialogue between the pair. Unwilling to believe the "surface logic" of Jason's decision to remarry, Medea reproaches him for using "his clever tongue to decorate/His crimes with pretty words." If his reasons were true, she asks, why did he not tell her beforehand and enlist her support? Wasn't the problem rather that he couldn't face old age married to a barbarian wife?

To her recriminations Jason consistently asserts that it was only concern for the children's future that motivated his plans. He asserts that Medea should be grateful for this, and that she has only herself to blame for her banishment. Even so, he promises to provide for her needs and the children's, and to give her letters of introduction to his influential friends. Medea flatly refuses his offers. The argument ends on a grim note, with each promising the other they will suffer for their decisions.

The choral ode which follows this episode praises the virtue of moderation in matters of love. It laments the fact that Medea is condemned to see the world, but never again her home, and hopes that someone will open his doors to her.

Analysis

Here, for the first time, we meet the famed hero of the Argonauts, ironically presented by means of a domestic dispute. But in Euripides' hands, this marital argument is anything but petty. Through it Euripidies is able to illustrate some of the central issues of concern to Greeks of his time.

Now the attempts at rhetorical manipulation seem to be on Jason's side. He is the one presenting specious arguments in the face of Medea's bald presentation of distinctly un–pretty facts. In her impassioned account of their history together, she does not gloss over the horror of her own deeds—but neither does she accept full responsibility for them. Her long account incorporates a rather faithful version of the legend itself.

Immediately, Jason counters with the somewhat feeble argument, new to the story, that the escape of the Argo was due solely to Aphrodite's assistance. While this argument completely discounts Medea's aid, Jason then contradicts himself by begrudgingly granting that Medea did provide help. But he demeans her and aggrandizes himself by claiming this aid was motivated by her blind passion for him. He then further insults her by suggesting she should, in fact, be the grateful one. She now has the pleasure of living among the civilized Greeks. He diminishes her objections to his marriage with the facile "the marriage irks you./Isn't that like a woman?"

But it is his rationale for his pending marriage that Medea takes most to task. She refuses to accept that he was motivated solely out of concern for her and the children, repeatedly pointing out the betrayal, on both personal and moral levels, that his marriage represents:

> I cannot trust you now. Nor can I understand
> What you believe in—do you think the gods
> That used to govern us no longer do?
> You seem to imagine the moral law has changed—
> But even you must realize you've not kept your word.
> (30)

Their argument ends, as noted above, with each of them direly predicting the other will regret his or her decision. The match is a draw at this point. This battle is not just between a powerful and wronged woman and her ambitious and faithless husband; it is also between two opposing philosophical principles which can be broadly characterized as passion vs. reason, or heart vs. mind. Reconciling these principles to co-exist harmoniously was a central preoccupation of the Greek philosophers of Euripides' time. It is a view which finds expression in the choral ode which ends the scene.

In Medea we see the consequences of a passion untempered by self–control, as amply demonstrated in her own account of her early days with Jason. Perhaps living among the Corinthians and trying to fit in with them has taught Medea something of self–mastery, as some of the earlier passages in the play suggest. But this recently acquired skill, quickly deserts her when her sense of justice is violated. Hence her many diatribes against her "enemies," and Creon's fear for what they represent.

On the other hand, Jason represents the opposite end of the continuum between passion and reason. Though he admits he "cannot imagine hating" Medea, his calculated ambition prevents him from honoring the promises he made to her. He is cool, apparently in firm control of his own emotions, and ultimately completely interested only in himself and his anticipated royal bloodline. If Euripides cannot permit Medea to win this round, due to the depths of her passion, neither can he permit Jason to win because of his unwillingness to admit any faults of his own.

The Chorus provides some form of mediation in this debate, arguing for the Greek ideal of moderation in matters concerning the heart. It acknowledges both that Medea's problems are due to her excessive love for Jason, and that his are due in part to the hypocrisy of this self–proclaimed reasonable man, who is violating the moral laws of marriage. They seek instead a middle ground where the passions of love can find their proper expression:

> Eros at times comes over us too strong,
> Which wrecks our reputation
> And leads us into doing wrong.
> But if she comes in moderation,
> No goddess can delight you
> As much as Aphrodite...
> ...I hope that she respects
> The quiet of all peaceful marriage beds
> And judges right whose bodies and whose heads
> To stir with sex. (34–35)

While Medea is chastized for her prior over–devotion to Jason, he too is criticized for his own adulterous intents, poorly masked by his alleged concern for his family's future. Medea's passion is untempered by compassion; Jason's practical planning lacks the spark of human concern. Both will prove ultimately destructive to themselves and others.

Study Questions

1. Why does Jason tell Medea she should count herself lucky to have received only exile?

2. What does Medea call the "worst disease of human minds"?

3. How does the fact that they have had children together enter into Medea's argument?

4. Whom does Jason credit with the rescue of the Argonauts?

5. Why does Jason say Medea got more than she gave in the story of their time together?

6. What is Jason's justification for deciding to marry the Corinthian princess?

7. What is the point Medea uses effectively to destroy the "surface logic" of Jason's plans?

8. What does Medea suspect is really the motivation for this marriage?

9. Why does Medea refuse Jason's offer of help?

10. What are two themes covered in the choral ode which ends this episode?

Answers

1. According to Jason, Medea has repeatedly cursed the king, an act of treason which could have resulted in death.

2. The "worst disease of human minds," to Medea, is "having a blank where shame should be," by which she refers to Jason's arrogance in facing her after betraying her.

3. Medea claims that she could have forgiven Jason's wandering if they had been childless, but as it is, he has broken faith with the children as well.

4. Jason credits Aphrodite, and only Aphrodite, with saving that expedition.

5. Jason believes that, living among the Greeks, Medea has learned what it is to live under just rulers, compared to the rule of despots in her native land. Further, she is famous throughout Greece for her role in that adventure, and without it no one would have ever heard of her.

6. He claims that he wants to ensure a better future for all concerned, by allying the two families together, and that he wishes to assure all of his children the benefits of his royal descent, denied him in his own family.

7. Medea claims that if he'd been truly honest, he would have discussed these plans with her and secured her approval before proceeding with them.

8. Medea suspects that Jason does not want to grow old married to a barbarian, while the glories of his former reputation fade into the past.

9. Medea refuses Jason's offer, saying she would not profit from the gifts of a "bad man."

10. One theme is the virtue of moderation and self–control in matters of love; another is the pain of exile being worse than that of death.

Suggested Essay Topics

1. Though Medea has not been able to convince Jason to see her side of things in this scene, she nevertheless shows Jason to be something of a hypocrite. How does their debate reveal Jason in this light? Specifically address the way he responds to her accusations of his role in their prior life together, and discuss his willingness to allow the children to be banished in light of his claims that he was acting only on their behalf.

2. How does Euripides use the debate between Medea and Jason, and the choral response to that debate, to illustrate conventional views about the relative merits of passion vs. reason? In both the content and tone of Medea's speeches, how does she come to represent the side of passion? Similarly, how are Jason's arguments structured to reveal the problems of too–cold reason? Finally, how does the Chorus serve as a kind of mediator in the philosophical issues raised by the couple?

Medea
Third Episode: Medea and Aegeus

New Character:

Aegeus: *King of Athens, longtime friend of Medea*

Summary

Aegeus, the King of Athens, enters on his return from the oracle of Apollo at Delphi. There he asked for blessings and advice on how to relieve his childless state. Meeting Medea, he is concerned to see her looking "pale and strained."

Medea explains her situation to Aegeus, who is quite sympathetic. She asks for his help in providing sanctuary, in return for which she promises a cure for his problem. Aegeus agrees, on the

condition that he need provide only sanctuary, not help in her escape. Medea further asks him to swear by the Earth, by her grandfather the sun god, and by all the gods that he will not turn her over to any of her enemies, no matter how tempted he may be. Aegeus so swears, and receives the travel blessing of the Chorus as he leaves.

Having secured a refuge, Medea now begins to make her plans. She will convince Jason she has had a change of heart, then send to the bride, gifts which she will poison so that whoever touches them will die horribly. This will be easy, but a harder task awaits her. She declares she must also kill her children, as the way to hurt Jason most. The Chorus is horrified by this turn of events, but Medea will not be dissuaded. She sends the Nurse off to fetch Jason so that she may put her plans in motion.

The episode ends with the Chorus meditating on the glory of Athens and wondering about the fate that awaits it for harboring this "unclean" murderess. They end on the hopeful note that in the final moment, Medea will not be able to carry out her awful plan.

Analysis

Structurally, the episode between Medea and Aegeus marks a key turning point in the play. Up to now, Medea's reactions to her situation have resided in the realm of her emotions, and a definite plan has not yet taken shape in her mind because she is not sure that she will be able to escape safely. With the promise of safe harbor in Athens, she can now turn her thoughts to strategizing her revenge.

Her address to the Chorus, in which she shares this strategy, is also an important structural component of the play. In her first address, as we have seen, she has tried mightily to keep her passions in check, using persuasive words to stimulate their own feelings of injustice and win them to her side. In the second address, following her meeting with Creon, a more sinister side emerges, as she begins to ponder the best way to kill the king and his daughter. Finally, the full horror of her determination is revealed when she includes her own children in her murderous plans. Thus, in these three addresses Euripides accelerates the emotional impact of the action of the play as a whole, through the increasing intensity of Medea's commitment to her vengeance.

Thematically, the scene is also important for several reasons. First, it further fleshes out the character of Medea, by showing her to be the honored friend of a respected king. Aegeus does not hesitate in confiding to her the nature of his problem, nor does he minimize her unhappiness about her own situation. The feeling in the *stychomythia* between them, as Aegeus relates the rather enigmatic advice of the oracle, is similar to that adopted by a doctor and her patient, as Medea asks a series of questions designed to elicit a better understanding of Aegeus' situation. That he so readily accepts her offer to help him in return for sanctuary is further evidence of his confidence in her abilities.

Second, in Aegeus's problem—growing old without heirs—we are reminded again of the "children theme" in the play, and of the seriousness of the fate of a king who dies heirless. Aegeus does not suspect, however, that his own desire to escape that fate removes the last obstacle to Medea's plans to impose it on Jason.

Finally, in the response of the Chorus to Medea's address, Euripides introduces a significant shift in their attitude toward her. Where before they have been only full of sympathy for her plight and only too willing to blame Jason for his part in it, now they begin to qualify their support. It is important to note that this withdrawal is couched in terms of fear for the future of Athens, the larger audience the Chorus addresses. Opening with a sort of tribute to the virtues embodied in this ideal city, living in harmony under the sweetly scented breezes of the breath of Aphrodite, the Chorus paints Medea's place within it in harshly contrasting terms:

> So how will that city of holy rivers
> That country hospitable to friends,
> Take in the murderess of her sons,
> Unclean among its citizens? (41)

The audience can only wonder at how Aegeus' hospitality will be repaid, although it would have known from legend that once in Athens, Medea will attempt the murder of his beloved son, Theseus. Euripedes asks us to consider whether any city can be safe from the principles of unchecked passion and vengence that Medea represents.

But at the end of their ode, the Chorus (and perhaps the audience as well) is still hopeful of a change of heart. After all, Medea has convinced the chorus that she is truly one of them, and none of them could consider such a deed. Thus the episode ends poised at the crucial moment of the play, and the central question which will occupy its remainder is whether or not Medea will justify the Chorus' remaining faith in her.

Study Questions

1. Why is the Athenian king Aegeus in Corinth?

2. How does Aegeus greet Medea?

3. When Aegeus first learns of Medea's situation, he tells her simply to forget Jason. What causes him to re–evaluate?

4. What does Medea ask of Aegeus?

5. What two reasons does Aegeus give for wishing to help Medea?

6. What does Medea plan to say to Jason when next she sees him?

7. What are the gifts Medea plans to send the bride?

8. Who is to deliver these gifts to the princess?

9. What does Medea say is the way to earn respect in Greece?

10. When the Chorus first tries to dissuade Medea from killing her children, why does she tell them it's necessary that she do so?

Answers

1. He has just been to the oracle of Apollo at Delphi, seeking a cure for his childlessness.

2. Aegeus greets Medea with a wish for happiness, as befitting a friend.

3. Aegeus seems to take more seriously the fact that Jason's lust is not simply for another woman, but for the power of a royal marriage.

4. Medea desires Aegeus' royal protection once she arrives in Athens.

5. First, he wishes to help her because he believes it would please the gods to do so. Second, he wishes to take advantage of her promise to cure his problem in reward for his aid.

6. Medea plans to tell him she wishes to reconcile with him, for the best interests of everyone. Further, she will ask that the children be allowed to stay in Corinth with him.

7. Medea plans to present the princess with a poisoned robe and wreath, or crown, which will cause her and anyone who touches her in them to die.

8. The children are to bring them to the princess as a gesture of Medea's reconciliation.

9. Respect is earned by being "gentle to friends, implacable to foes."

10. Medea claims that killing her children is the way to hurt Jason most.

Suggested Essay Topics

1. By the end of this episode, we have a rather more complete picture of the character of Medea. Write an essay on the multiple dimensions of this character, as drawn by Euripides in the episodes leading up to and including this one. Cite examples from what is said about her, what she says about herself, and what is revealed in her speeches to both the Chorus and the other characters in the play.

2. Comment on the ways Euripides was effective in keeping the theme of "the children" foremost in the minds of the audience, starting with the Nurse's fears for them in the prologue and continuing through each episode as they are mentioned. Include in your discussion their dual role as both children, per se, and as being necessary to the aims of a kingdom.

Medea
Fourth Episode: Medea and Jason

Summary

The Nurse returns with Jason, who listens to Medea's false plea for forgiveness. She claims she has thought over his arguments, found them sound, and sanctions the marriage. When the children enter she has a momentary stab of anguish, but she justifies her tears as part of the emotion of the moment.

Jason responds positively to this ruse, telling his children he will continue to see to their needs while they are away, so that they may return someday to Corinth prepared to take their place with their new brothers. At this, Medea begins to weep again, this time explaining that the talk of their future has saddened her.

She then proceeds to ask Jason to intercede on their children's behalf, asking Creon to allow them to stay on without her. When Jason expresses doubt, Medea seizes the chance to suggest Jason start by convincing the princess to do the asking. She then "sweetens the deal" by offering to give the princess gifts made of precious gold that were orginally given to Medea by her ancestor, the Sun god.

Jason accepts the offer, and allows the children to accompany him to the palace to present the gifts. They and their Tutor leave with Jason. Meanwhile, the Chorus, who has been watching with growing misgivings, is left with the certainty that now there will be no turning back. Their ending ode is filled with dire predictions of the disaster that will befall Jason, his intended, and his children; and the doom that awaits Medea because of her response to Jason's betrayal.

Analysis

This episode and the ones coming after it are short and quickly paced. Medea's meeting with Jason is a masterpiece of willfullness and self–control, shaken only briefly when she is reminded that the hopes for their children's future, that she and Jason discuss, will be irrevocably dashed by her own hand.

Harking back to the same strategies of the fawning hypocrite she used with Creon, Medea begins by abasing herself as an "obstinate, silly woman" for not seeing the wisdom of Jason's plan. In a complete reversal of the truth, she accuses herself of not being able to plan ahead and letting her anger overrule her reason. She has acted, she says, "childishly," but asks Jason to see this for what it is, womanly "frailty," not "wickedness."

While the audience is not fooled by this false submissiveness, Jason surely is. One wonders, really, how well Jason could know his wife, that he could so readily accept her "act" of contrition. Perhaps this is Euripides' way of subtly suggesting, as the Chorus more blatantly will, that Jason has brought his doom upon himself. His lust for power, it seems, has blinded him to the very real power that resides in the person of his wife, whom he so disastrously underestimates.

But Medea's resolve is not so firm that she is not pierced by the knowledge of what is to come. Weeping openly in front of the children and Jason, she is hard pressed to justify her tears, offering the feeble excuses that women are "naturally given to tears," and that "life is so uncertain."

Consider the stage direction implied by the following lines of Medea's:

> So take his hand, his right hand—O my dears!
> I thought of the pain the future hides from us.
> O children! may you live long years like this
> Holding out your arms... (42)

Here Euripides provides one of the most chilling tableaux in stage history—of the children, arms trustingly outstretched to the father who will take them on the first steps of their deathbound journey. The Chorus and Medea herself are moved by the sight, as indicated by their weeping in the following lines.

Some critics have made compelling arguments for the case that these tears of Medea's are not genuine, that they are in fact further evidence of her calculating ability to manipulate the feelings of others. Seen from the standpoint of the play's structure as a whole, however, these momentary lapses of Medea's resolve anticipate the longer debate she will have with herself in the next episode. Together, both serve to heighten the dramatic tension as the play proceeds. Will she or won't she kill her children?

At this point, the Chorus provides a clue. When Jason goes off with the children, bearing the gifts that, if accepted, will bring the ruin of his dreams, the Chorus' despair is complete: "Now there's no hope, not any more, for the children's lives./They are walking at this moment towards death" (45).

Each succeeding verse anticipates the stages of the disaster: the destruction of the princess, Jason's suffering, and Medea's final, unhappy act. Jason's readiness to accept Medea's false humility, to believe her mendacious assessment of his superior wisdom, has sealed his fate. The structure of the choral ode here traces the consequences of that folly, and will be echoed, as we shall see, in the structure of the succeeding episodes.

Study Questions

1. What are three examples of Medea's false self–reproaching in her opening speech to Jason?

2. What motivates Medea's first bout of weeping?

3. Why does Jason say he doesn't blame Medea for her angrier moods?

4. Does Jason give any evidence that he has considered keeping the children in Corinth with him?

5. What motivates Medea's second round of tears?

6. What is the real reason that Medea asks that the children be allowed to stay?

7. How has Medea come by the gifts of the robe and wreath?

8. When Jason balks at Medea's disposal of her inheritance, how does she convince him to take it?

9. What are Medea's instructions to the children?

10. In the choral ode which ends this episode, who does the Chorus seem to blame for the coming destruction, and why?

Answers

1. Medea berates herself for her stubbornness in not acting on Jason's good advice. She blames her inability to curb her temper for her short–sightedness; and she admits she was acting childishly out of womanly frailty.

2. Medea is moved to tears by the act of handing her children over to Jason.

3. He says it's natural for a woman to be angry when her husband takes a new wife.

4. No, it is apparent from his first response to Medea that Jason does not anticipate seeing the boys again until they are grown, and it is not until Medea directly asks him to keep them does he promise at least to try to intercede on their behalf.

5. Medea is moved to tears again at Jason's dream of his children returning to Corinth after they've reached the "full mark of manhood," as she knows the truth will be otherwise.

6. Although not made explicit in the dialogue, this request bolsters Medea's claim that she has had a complete change of heart regarding her belief in Jason's wisdom over his marriage. The idea is that the innocent children should not be made to suffer the same consequences as their mother.

7. They were given to her family by their ancestral sun god, and taken with her from Colchis when she and Jason fled her homeland.

8. Medea reminds Jason of the saying that even gods can be swayed by gifts, and these precious articles will help him convince the princess to speak to her father on the children's behalf.

9. She tells them to beg the princess themselves not to be banished.

10. The Chorus blames Jason, because he has broken the law regarding his promises to Medea, and "married into power," thus unknowingly bringing on his own ruin.

Suggested Essay Topics

1. Though this is clearly Medea's play from start to finish, the role of Jason is an extremely important one. Given what he says and does, as well as what others say about him, has Euripides drawn him sympathetically? That is, is the audience meant to identify with him more strongly than with Medea at this point in the play? Support you argument with examples from the text.

2. Taken from the action of the play up to this episode, write an essay defending one or the other position regarding Medea's tears in this scene. Do you agree that they are genuine? Or do you hold the view that they are a mere device calculated to win Jason's sympathy? Again, support your argument with examples from Medea's previous actions and the Chorus' responses to them.

Medea
Fifth Episode: Medea, Tutor, and Children

Summary

The Tutor returns with the children and the news that they have been released from exile. Medea receives this news glumly, telling the Tutor that her mood is caused by sadness at the pending separation from her sons.

Left alone with her children in front of the female company of Nurse and Chorus, Medea vacillates between carrying out her plans and changing her mind. Twice she decides she cannot bear to murder them, and twice she renews her commitment to do so. In the end, she decides it is better for them to die at her hands than at the hands of her enemies, in revenge for her poisoning of the princess.

The Chorus then muses on the reasons for the desire to have children, when they bring as much pain as joy, and when Fate may cause them to die before their parents do.

Analysis

In this short but powerful episode, we see Medea searching her soul for the strength to carry out her plans. It is perhaps significant that this internal debate occurs before she learns of the outcome of her plan to murder the princess. This is the last time we see the human, maternal side of the woman who will later show no remorse for her horrible actions.

This human side is poignantly drawn. When the Tutor returns with the seemingly happy news that the princess has accepted the gifts and the children are granted a reprieve from exile, Medea's response is a bitter, "How cruel." Unaware of her real plans (which have been shared only with the women in the chorus), the Tutor assumes Medea is simply unable to bear being separated from her children. Her words in this part of the scene are filled with double meaning, in which we can trace the pattern of her thoughts, as well as the Tutor's misunderstanding of her real intent.

> MEDEA:
> How can I help it [weeping]?—when I think the gods
> And my own wicked thoughts have worked to make
> this happen.

> TUTOR:
> Take heart; some day the boys will come to Athens
> And bring you back from exile, down to Corinth.

> MEDEA:
> Ah, before that, I shall bring others down.

> TUTOR:
> You're not the only woman to be separated
> From her children: we must learn to bear things lightly.

> MEDEA:
> I'll try to do so. But go in. Get the children
> Whatever they need—like any other day. (47)

Taking only the surface meaning of her words, the Tutor obeys. Left with her children, Medea agonizes over her decision. Still protective of their feelings, she carries on the illusion that her grief is over leaving them behind. In a long passage, she mourns over everything she will miss in their lives, all the maternal joys she must now sacrifice. Again, the double meaning is clear: while the audience knows the real source of her grief, the children are spared this horrible knowledge, at least for a time. This is a powerful example of dramatic irony, created when the audience knows more about what's happening on stage than do the characters.

But if we are content to rest securely (however uncomfortably) with our "inside knowledge," Euripides is not. The remainder of Medea's speech requires the audience to forgo this security and go along with Medea. At first, it seems as though all might be saved. Medea decides to take the boys with her, because after all, killing them to hurt their father would still mean that "all his pain would be nothing to mine."

Just as our hopes are raised, however, they are immediately dashed again. In the very next line Medea takes herself to task for being cowardly, and vows that her "hand's not going to weaken." But suddenly she changes her mind, deciding to let the children remain in Corinth. And then once again, this time finally, she acknowledges that to do so would almost certainly be to turn them over to the hands of her enemies. Her final action is to smother her children with kisses, in a wrenching moment of love and loss, before she sends them into the palace to seal their fate.

But Medea's debate with herself over what she has set out to do is more than an illustration of maternal anguish calculated to remind us of Medea–the–woman. Witnessing this anguish, we also come to understand the inevitability of the children's fate, rooted in Medea's character and her prior actions. Because her gifts have been accepted, she knows the princess will soon be dead, and that to leave her children behind will be to expose them to the revenge of her enemies. On the other hand, to take them with her would mean that she has not fulfilled her own desire for revenge over Jason by leaving him heirless in his dreams of empire. Though she is fully aware that what she is about to do is evil and wrong, she cannot escape the force of her own character.

> But the rage of my heart is stronger than my reason—
> That is the cause of all man's foulest crimes. (48)

One might think at this point the moderation–loving Chorus would be moved once again to meditate on its virtues, but curiously they do not. Nor do they ever address Medea directly again. Instead, Euripides has them asking profound and unanswerable questions about the human desire to procreate, persistent in the face of earthly hardship and divine caprice.

It is as though the Chorus, impressed by the inevitability of the children's fate, can no longer bear to contemplate it: choosing to mull over the general human condition rather than to dwell on the fate of these particular representatives. But this is only a brief reprieve, to be shattered conclusively by the Messenger's report in the coming scene.

Study Questions

1. How does Medea react to the Tutor's news from the palace, and how does he in turn respond to this?

2. In Medea's recounting of all the things she'll miss by giving up her sons, we can learn something about ancient familial traditions. What mother's rituals, for example, will Medea not be able to perform for her sons?

3. Similarly, what filial obligation will her sons not be able to perform for her?

4. What first causes Medea to re–think her original plan to kill her children?

5. What makes her renew her resolve after this?

6. In the end, what decides the children's fate?

7. The children are present on stage the whole time Medea argues with herself about them. Is there ever any specific reference in her words as to what her final decision means?

8. How is Medea's exchange with the Tutor an example of "dramatic irony"?

9. In the opening lines of the choral passage, how does the fe-

male Chorus characterize the gender–specific nature of philosophical debate it is about to enter into?

10. What is the substance of this debate?

Answers

1. Medea begins to weep, which surprises the Tutor. He thinks she's overreacting.

2. She will not be able to decorate their marriage beds, nor "hold the wedding torches" over them.

3. They will not be able to prepare her body for the grave when she dies.

4. Medea's heart is softened by the sight of their "shining faces," smiling up at her.

5. When Medea thinks of her enemies mocking her and going unpunished, she hardens her heart again.

6. Medea knows that they will suffer at the hands of her enemies if she does not kill them herself.

7. An alert child would have good reason to suspect something unpleasant was afoot, but there is no overt mention of actually killing them in this speech.

8. Dramatic irony occurs when the audience knows more than a character or characters do. In this case, the audience knows more about why Medea is weeping than the Tutor does, because he has not heard any of Medea's plans. Unlike him, we are thus able to understand the scene on more than one level.

9. By "asking, as men might ask," about the question of having children, the Chorus characterizes such debates as more conventionally the domain of men than women.

10. The Chorus questions the wisdom of the desire for having children, since it so difficult to raise them, since they might turn out to be bad adults, and finally, since they might end up dying before their parents do, causing them grief and worry for nothing.

Suggested Essay Topics

1. Comment on the dual purpose of Medea's soul searching in this episode, as both an illustration of her more humane instincts, as well as a means to show why the children's fate is sealed. How does she evidence her maternal feelings for her children? And how, ultimately, does she overcome them?

2. The presence of the children throughout Medea's monologue ensures the dramatic irony within it. Analyze this speech to show how Euripides was able to let the audience in on her thoughts, without giving them fully away to their victims.

Medea
Sixth Episode: The Messenger

New Character:

Messenger: *one of Jason's servants, arriving from the royal palace*

Summary

A servant arrives from the royal house, breathless with news of what he has witnessed there. Medea responds with delighted anticipation, asking him to tell his tale slowly, as it will please her doubly to learn her victims have died horribly.

The Messenger complies, with a detailed account of all he has seen. He describes how the princess, aloof at first, was convinced by Jason to receive his sons and their gifts, and to release them from their sentence of exile. Delighted with those presents, she immediately proceeded to put them on, admiring herself in the mirror. He graphically recounts in each macabre detail the "long, long moments" of excruciating pain, as the princess was made to suffer a truly gruesome death.

The Messenger goes on to relate the equally gruesome death of her father Creon, who threw himself in despair on her lifeless body, only to become horribly fused himself to the poisoned gar-

ments she wore. He ends his tale with a brief meditation on the
unhappiness of mortals, and their vulnerability to the gods.

Medea immediately reconfirms her resolve to kill her children
before it can happen by "some unkinder hand," calling herself to
courage in the face of softer memories as she makes her way into
her own house. After she goes, the Chorus calls upon the gods of
earth and sky to stay Medea's hand. After all, her sons are also related by blood through her to the sun god. Their ode closes with a
further lament for the fate of both the children and their mother,
whose crushing "weight of anger" has driven her to this end and
risked the further wrath of the gods.

Analysis

In most of the extant Greek tragedies (though not all—see for
example Sophocles' *Ajax*), violent deaths occur off–stage, and require that they be made known to the audience through the report
of some kind of messenger. In the case of *Medea*, the actor playing
the part of the Messenger would have reason to covet his role, as
it's difficult to imagine a gorier tale.

This tale is made all the more horrible by the account of happy
reconciliation and girlish vanity that precedes it. Through the
Messenger's eyes, we too can see the group of servants, kissing the
children in their relief that their parents had finally patched things
up. We watch with him to see if the princess will accept the children and their gifts, or turn them away. We see how she could barely
resist the beauty of these gifts, hurrying to try them on as soon as
Jason and the children left. We share the view of her preening in
front of the mirror, turning this way and that for full effect. And we
watch, horrified, to see this all–to–human scene turn into one of
monstrously inhuman proportions.

No paraphrase of what follows in the Messenger's speech
would do justice to Euripides' own words, and the reader is urged
to encounter the full force of them in the text. Suffice it to say that
Medea's hope that the princess and Creon died "horribly" has been
more than amply fulfilled. By the end of the reported scene, the
Messenger and all the witnesses have been reduced to tears of relief that the awful suffering is over.

Some scholars have criticized this scene for introducing a

melodramatic note that is out of keeping with the dignity of classic tragedy. This may be so, but only if taken out of the context of all that has come before. To be sure, Medea shows absolutely no remorse at the suffering she has caused, exhibiting in its place a morbid fascination to hear every bloody detail, and she is only more resolved in her determination to carry out the rest of her plans. This stands in sharp contrast to her reaction to the earlier report of the Tutor, which motivates the most human self–presentation Medea makes in the course of the play.

If Medea had been nothing but a villainess all along, if she had marched forward without once looking back from beginning to end, then we would have justification for calling the play a melodrama. As it is, we have seen her human side, the maternal side that is in fact a stronger opponent than Jason and Creon together, for it alone might have had the power to make her change her course. That we have witnessed this mighty struggle within her can help us to see the more subtle dimensions of a tragic heroine, more than a merely melodramatic one, even if we can only lament with the Chorus over the outcome of that dubious victory.

Study Questions

1. What causes the Messenger's haste from the palace?

2. How does Medea initially respond to the news that Creon and the princess are dead?

3. Why does Medea exhort the Messenger to tell his tale slowly?

4. To whom does the Messenger compare the princess, when he speaks of the honor he and the other servants pay her?

5. According to the Messenger, how did the princess first react upon seeing Medea's children?

6. What made the princess change her mind?

7. How much time elapsed between the bestowal of the gifts and the death of the princess?

8. How did Creon die?

9. To what does the Messenger compare human life, after he has completed his tale?

10. How does the Chorus judge the way the gods have treated Jason?

Answers

1. The fact and manner of the two deaths have necessitated Medea's immediate escape, and he wishes to warn her.

2. She calls it a beautiful message, and promises to regard the Messenger forever as her benefactor and friend.

3. She says it will give her twice as much delight to hear that the pair died horribly.

4. The Messenger says the servants honor the princess as they once honored Medea.

5. She turned her face away, in anger and disgust.

6. She was softened by Jason's appeal on their behalf, and by the incomparable beauty of the gifts.

7. The poison began to take effect almost immediately, but the suffering ocurred over "long, long moments." In Greek tragedy, staged time almost always proceeds continuously, so the ordeal of the princess and Creon would have occurred during the previous episode, while Medea was debating over her plans.

8. Upon seeing what had become of his daughter, Creon threw himself on her body, thus exposing himself to the deadly poison as well. He was literally skinned alive.

9. The Messenger says human life is "nothing but a shadow," and anyone who thinks mortals can find happiness in it is wrong.

10. They maintain his punishment was deserved.

Suggested Essay Topics

1. Euripides chose to spread out the telling of what happened at the palace over two separate episodes, this one and the previous one. Why do you think this was dramatically necessary to the play? What would the effect be, for example, of

simply having the report come all at once, forcing Medea's hand without giving her (and the audience) the time to reflect over possible alternatives? Would the play suffer in any way from our not witnessing her soul–searching? Or do you think it would be strengthened by marching more quickly on to its conclusion?

2. In the last chapter we noted that the Chorus is no longer addressing itself directly to Medea, and in the final lyric of this episode they turn to the deities of the earth and sun. Examining the choral passages of this episode and the previous one, why do you think this is so? Is there any evidence that their support for Medea is weakening, or is it merely colored now by deeper concerns? What do they say that supports your conclusion?

Medea
Final Episode and Exodos

Summary

Off–stage the cries of the children are heard as they try to no avail to escape their mother's sword. Jason enters in haste from the royal palace, seeking to rescue his sons from the wrath of the Corinthians. From the Chorus, he learns the awful truth.

In despair, he rushes the palace doors, but Medea has already drawn her divine chariot up to its roof, bearing in it the bodies of the two boys. (The chariot had been given to her by the sun god, for her protection, and Jason cannot touch her while she is in it.) To Jason's long string of curses at what she has done, she replies only that the gods have been witness to the deeds he's done that have merited this revenge.

What follows is another example of *stychomythia* between Jason and Medea, as each tries to make the other feel even worse. But Jason's cries only ease Medea's pain. His final request— that he be allowed to have the bodies—is denied by Medea, who fears

their graves will be desecrated by her enemies. Instead, she will take them to Hera's temple in Corinth, where an annual celebration will be instituted in their honor. Then she will proceed to the house of Aegeus in Athens, under his promise of royal protection. She prophesies a humiliating and unheroic death for Jason.

The play ends on Jason's wish that he'd never met Medea, nor bore children with her, calling on the gods to witness his anguish.

Analysis

Having laid the groundwork for character and plot in all the previous episodes, Euripides does not linger long over the play's final moments. The children are quickly murdered (though not before we hear their pathetic cries), and the Chorus and Jason can do little more than wring their hands and raise their voices in powerless agony.

In this agony, however, two rather distinct views of Medea emerge. On the one hand, the Chorus compares her to Ino the only other woman in history to have done what Medea did. Ino was driven to insanity by the jealous wife of Zeus, and, after killing her sons, drowned herself. But no fewer than three times do they repeat: "Medea is not mad." There is no way for them to account for what she has done. The powers of sympathy they have been able to muster seem to desert them now.

Jason, on the other hand, can only assume that Medea must be entirely mad or utterly inhuman. He has brought her to Greece, the cradle of civilization, but her barbarism has prevailed. He calls her an "abominable thing," "a tiger, a savage, not a woman." She has a "monstrous spirit." A "sane woman," certainly a Greek woman, would never have acted as she has.

In Jason's words, ringing down the play's end, Euripides comes full circle with the imagery associated with Medea in the play's opening moments. Critic D.J. Conacher suggests this is part of Euripides' intent. Throughout the play, he argues, the dramatist has fleshed out the human character of the sorceress of legend, and chooses to end it with her transformation back into the "fiend" whose magical powers guarantee her safe escape.

This escape, convenient as it seems, has been regarded negatively by critics going as far back as Aristotle, who found it compromised the dramatic coherence of the events which preceded it. Others have found in it a device, characteristically Euripidean, for questioning the wisdom of the gods. If, as Jason and the Chorus have cried, her act is an abomination to the deities of the Earth and Sky, why would the Sun god have seemed to sanction it by providing the means of her escape? Still others have seen in her desire to escape retribution a final confirmation of her inherent and irredeemable wickedness.

Some feminist scholars have seen in Medea's successful escape a grim warning by Euripides to the men of Athens of the consequences of allowing women to have too much power. Others have interpreted it in exactly the opposite terms, that Euripides is, in fact, criticizing the patriarchal society that drives women to such desperate measures.

Because her escape is to the haven of civilized Athens, we can only imagine the shudder that might have collectively shaken the members of the play's original audience, citizens of that fair city, threatened by the barbarous intent of multiple enemies (Corinth among them) in this, the first year of the disastrous Pelopponesian War.

Whether Euripides intended his play to be an anti–Corinthian commentary, a critique of gender politics, or a creative dramatization of a widely recognized legend, can never be fully known. What is certain is that the drama he constructed, and the unforgettable characters he drew, continue thousands of years later to provoke debate and discussion among scholars, theatre practitioners, and audiences alike.

Study Questions

1. Why is Jason's entrance in this scene another example of dramatic irony at work?

2. Why is Jason trying to find his children?

3. Where does Medea appear in this scene?

4. Why is Medea protected while in the chariot?

5. Where are the children?

6. Which of Medea's previous crimes does Jason choose to

illustrate her wickedness?

7. How does Medea reply to Jason's accusations?

8. Who does Medea maintain "began this agony"?

9. Why does Medea deny Jason's request to take the boys' bodies?

10. How does Medea prophesy Jason will die?

Answers

1. Jason's entrance contains a measure of dramatic irony because he does not yet know, as we do, that the sons he is seeking are already dead. His unawareness is short–lived, however.

2. He fears, as does Medea, that the Corinthians will kill them in revenge for Medea's murder of their king and princess.

3. Although there are no explicit stage directions, it is clear from her words that she is in her chariot. It is traditionally held that this would have been placed on the roof of the outdoor playing area, a space called the *theologeion*, or "stage of the gods."

4. The chariot was a gift to her from her grandfather, the sun god, given to her especially for her protection. No one can harm her while she is within it.

5. Medea has brought their bodies with her into the chariot.

6. Jason refers to her murder of her brother during her escape with Jason from Colchis.

7. She replies that the gods are witnesses to the reasons for actions, and that her victims were not fated to go on living— and laughing—at her expense.

8. She places the blame securely on Jason's shoulders.

9. She fears their graves will be dug up by her enemies.

10. He will be crushed to death by a rotting timber from his ship, the Argo.

Suggested Essay Topics

1.   In the play's closing moments, Medea has conclusively won her victory over Jason, ruining his plans for building a new royal bloodline. In your opinion, with which of the opposing characters are we meant to identify in this scene— Medea, whose reasons for doing the unthinkable have been repeated throughout the play, or with Jason, who can be said to have paid too dearly for his ambition? Or is the answer really not clearly one or the other? Provide support for your opinion with relevant material from the play.

2.   Which of the following two views regarding Medea's escape do you prefer: 1) that indeed, as the Chorus has suggested earlier in the play, all of nature has turned upside down, and even the gods are sanctioning evil on Earth; or 2) that Medea's desire to escape the consequences of her actions proves once and for all the irredeemable corruptness of Medea's character? Or, do you hold an alternative view? Provide support for your conclusions from the text itself.

SECTION THREE

Electra

Mythological Background to Electra

Euripides' *Electra* isolates one incident in an epic tale of the curse that follows the royal House of Atreus from generation to generation. According to legend, Atreus fought with his brother, Thyestes, for rule of the kingdom of Mycenae (called Argos in Euripides' play) in southern Greece. Thyestes seduced his brother's wife, Aerope, and together they plotted against Atreus. Atreus prevailed, however, and in revenge murdered and cooked up Thyestes' two older children, serving them to their father at a banquet.

Later, Thyestes' other son, Aigisthos, seduced Clytemnestra, wife of Atreus' son Agamemnon, who had followed his father as king of Mycenae, and then left his kingdom to lead the Greek expedition against Troy. Agamemnon sacrificed his daughter, Iphigenia, at the outset of the war, in the belief that by so doing he could secure victory for the Greeks. The Greeks did win, but only after many lives were lost and the holy shrines of Troy destroyed. When the war was finally over, Agamemnon returned home with the prophetess, Cassandra, as part of his war booty. Agamemnon's murder of Iphigenia and subsequent return with a beautiful mistress did nothing to endear him to Clytemnestra. She and her lover Aigisthos murdered Agamemnon in revenge.

Then begins another cycle in the saga of blood vengeance. Clytemnestra's other two children, Orestes and Electra, could not forgive their mother for murdering their father. Fearing their eventual revenge, Clytemnestra and Aigisthos separated them as children and sent Orestes far away, believing he could cause no harm to the new household. However, as young adults the two reunited, after Orestes had been ordered by Apollo to kill their mother and her lover.

Finally, fearing human retribution for his act of matricide, and pursued by the vengeful Furies, Orestes appealed for relief to Athena, goddess of wisdom. In response, she established a court of justice—the foundation of Athenian democracy—which eventually exonerated him. Thus, the curse on the House of Atreus was finally broken.

Master List of Characters

Farmer—*Electra's husband.*

Electra—*Daughter of Clytemnestra and Agamemnon, sister of Orestes.*

Orestes—*Electra's brother.*

Pylades—*Orestes' friend and son of Orestes' protector Strophios.*

Chorus—*Young, single peasant women from the rural area where Electra and her husband live.*

Old Man—*Former tutor of Agamemnon.*

Messenger—*Servant of Orestes.*

Clytemnestra—*Widow/murderess of Agamemnon; mother of Electra and Orestes.*

Dioskouroi—*Demi-gods Castor and Polydeukes, sons of Zeus and half-brothers of Clytemnestra.*

Others—*Farmer's servants, attendants to Orestes and Pylades, Trojan slave women attending Clytemnestra.*

Summary of the Play

The play opens outside the humble farmhouse where Electra lives a chaste life with her peasant husband. Born a princess to the kingdom of Argos (or Mycenae), Electra chafes at the injustice of her arranged low-status marriage, which denies her all the rights and comforts of her royal blood. But what rankles worse is her unfulfilled wish for revenge against her mother and stepfather, who had conspired to murder her father Agamemnon. It has been seven years since she and her brother Orestes were separated from each other, in order to avert the threat they represent to the new royal household. Electra longs to be reunited with Orestes so that they may avenge their father's death.

A stranger appears at the farmhouse, and after misreading several unmistakeable signs that it is indeed Orestes, Electra finally, joyfully, recognizes him, and the two make their plans. Orestes is to waylay and murder his stepfather Aigisthos as he prepares for a ritual feast. Electra is to lure her estranged mother, Clytemnestra, to her cottage on the ruse that she has just given birth and needs her mother's help.

While awaiting Clytemnestra's arrival, news comes from Orestes that he has succeeded in his bloody mission. Soon he and his companion, Pylades, return with Aigisthos' corpse, and Electra reminds him that there is one more murder to be done. Orestes balks. After all, Clytemnestra is still their mother, and he is tempted to ignore the Apollonian prophecy that she will die at his hands. Electra, however, is firm in her belief that their father must be avenged, and finally wins the argument by appealing to Orestes' manhood.

Clytemnestra arrives, full of motherly concern and hopeful of a reconciliation with her daughter. Electra picks an argument with her, which allows us to hear Clytemnestra's side of the story. She describes her grief over the death of her beloved daughter, Iphigenia, who was sacrificed by her husband Agamemnon, and her humiliation when Agamemnon flaunted his new mistress. Electra is unmoved, and brings her mother into the cottage, where she and Orestes slit her throat.

After the deed is committed, they carry their mother's body out, cover it gently with Orestes' cloak, and pray that the sorrows of their house will be ended. But they still have to face the consequences of their crime. The Dioskouroi, demi–gods representing their father Zeus, appear, having witnessed the murder from on high. In typically Euripidean fashion, they proclaim Clytemnestra's death to have been just, but the deed which caused it unjust.

As a result, Orestes is to be prevented from ever ascending the throne of Argos, and must travel to Athens, where trial and eventual acquittal await him. As for Electra, she is to marry Orestes' friend Pylades, the farmer receiving suitable reward for his loss. Thus the play ends as it began, with Electra and her beloved brother separated again, this time forever.

Estimated Reading Time

Reading time will depend on the translation used. Generally allow two to three hours for a close reading. Like *Medea,* and most Greek tragedies, the tightly paced action reads best in one sitting. If you wish to break it up, you may do so by reading through the end of the scene in which Electra and Orestes make their plans and Orestes leaves to execute his part of them. In the Lembke and Reckford translation, this corresponds to line 724, and occurs almost exactly midway through the play.

Electra
Prologue and Parados

New Characters:

Farmer: *Electra's husband*

Electra: *daughter of Clytemnestra, sister of Orestes*

Orestes: *Electra's brother, returning from exile*

Pylades: *Orestes' traveling companion*

Chorus: *rural women of Argos*

Summary

The Farmer delivers the prologue, which recounts the events that have led up to his unlikely marriage to the royal maiden, Electra, daughter of Clytemnestra and Agamemnon. When her father returned home from victory against Troy, he was killed by his wife and her new lover, Aigisthos. Fearing that his stepchildren would grow up to avenge their father, Aigisthos would have killed Orestes, but an old tutor smuggled him off to be raised by a man

named Strophios.

Electra was kept at home, courted by the princes of the land, but Aigisthos refused to give her hand to any of them, fearing she would bear noble sons to do the work of revenge for her. Afraid that this might happen anyway, he would have killed her too, if not for Clytemnestra's intervention. Instead, he offered a price on Orestes' head to anyone who could bring him back from exile; and he married Electra off to a peasant so that her children would have no claim to the throne. Though married, the Farmer has not consummated the marriage out of respect for his high–born wife.

Electra enters, carrying a water jug and crying to the heavens over the circumstances to which her mother's treachery has reduced her. As they leave for the fields, Orestes and Pylades enter surreptitiously. Orestes tells how he has recently been ordered by Apollo to return home to avenge his father's murder. Having just visited his father's tomb, he now reveals his two–fold plan, which is to murder his father's murderer without being caught, and to find his sister Electra.

The men hide themselves when Electra re–enters, singing a dirge for her lost father, and calling for her brother to come home to help her avenge his death. She recounts how he was killed in his baths, the culmination of her mother's scheming while he was away. At first, Orestes thinks she is a servant, due to her humble dress, but her words clearly identify her as his long–lost sister.

A Chorus of young, unmarried women enters, singing and dancing to invite Electra to join them in an upcoming ritual for would–be brides. Against her refusal, they argue that the time for mourning has past, but Electra remains despondent. The Chorus ends with a comment that the woes of Electra, and indeed all of Greece, are due to one woman, Helen, whose abduction by Paris started the bloody Trojan War, in which so many Greeks lost their lives. (Helen is Clytemnestra's sister, considered to be the most beautiful woman in Greece.) Before she can respond, Electra spies Orestes and Pylades, and assumes they are strangers bent on harming them.

Analysis

Euripides was not the first, nor the last, to dramatize the legend of Orestes' and Electra's revenge on their murdered father. Its themes have found their way into more than a dozen plays of the twentieth century, suggesting the power of the underlying myth speaks as strongly to a modern audience as it did to the ancient Greeks.

When Euripides wrote his version (approximately 412 B.C.), it had already been dramatized at least one time before, as *The Libation Bearers* in Aeschylus' *Oresteia* trilogy (458 B.C.). Although the dating of the plays is uncertain, it seems likely that Sophocles, too, had already written his *Electra* before Euripides wrote his. Whether or not this is true, it seems certain that the popularity of Aeschylus' trilogy had guaranteed its familiarity among Athenian audiences, who must have been curious to see what Euripides would do with it.

Whether Euripides delivered or disappointed with his version has been a matter of scholarly debate. At one extreme are those who feel, as they do with his *Medea*, that Euripides' *Electra* is more melodramatic than tragically grand, and that its heroine is not likely to win our sympathy. At the other extreme are those who maintain that he realistically drew a portrait of a woman driven to near–madness with grief and deprivation at her mother's hands. Somewhere between the two is the view that Euripides drew his characters more subtly to continue his challenges to received wisdom.

In this view, Euripides plays the nobility of the peasant against the savagery of the nobles; the humanity of the victims against the brutality of their slayers; and the moral sanction of a divinely or–dered act of justice–as–concept against the horror of justice–in–action. In so doing, he critically re–examines the received notion, supported by Aeschylus and Sophocles both, that the ends justi–fied the means.

Euripides' inventiveness is evident in the first moments of the action, which he sets in the countryside that is Electra's new home. The action in the other two plays takes place at Agamemnon's tomb and at the royal palace, and in both of the other treatments Electra was still living at the palace under a kind of house arrest. In Euripides' version she is made to suffer, like her brother, an exile of sorts, and it is into her isolated world, far away from the palace of her youth, that the audience is drawn through the words of a humble Farmer.

This choice is not merely an artistic one, a change for the sake of change. Rather, removing the action of the play to the idyllic countryside makes for several interesting dramatic effects. First, this pleasant countryside will become the scene of a brutal double murder, and serves to throw those events into strong relief, as the curse of a royal house is made to play itself out, it seems, in even the humblest corners of the kingdom.

Second, this choice allows Euripides to highlight the isolation into which Electra has been forced, doubling the frustration of her inability to seek retribution for her father's death. We first meet her engaged in menial farm tasks, going for water from the spring like a servant, whereas the audience would have expected to see her carrying offerings to her father's grave. Her sympathetic husband reminds her, and us, of the depths to which she has sunk. This princess of a royal house is now hardly better than a slave. Every task reminds her of all she lost when she lost her father.

Some scholars have pointed out that there is an inherent contradiction between Electra's wailing words and the true reality of her position. In her first speech, she admits that her act of going for water is motivated less by necessity than by her desire to show the gods how Aigisthos has insulted her. When her husband gently reminds her that she does not have to do such heavy labor, she assumes an air of martyrdom in insisting that she play out her humble role. Later, when the Chorus invites her to share in their feasts, she complains that she has only rags to wear. Yet she declines their offer to provide her with suitable attire, refusing to shake off her cloak of ragged grief. This grief, it seems, is due as much for her murdered father as it is for her own loss of her heritage and the material comforts it would have provided her.

On the other hand, given her mother's role in her father's death (she is said to have planned it, leading her new lover Aigisthos to take him by surprise in his bath), the setting becomes a symbol of Electra's mental state. Even were she at home, she would still have no ally to turn to, not even her own mother. It is hard to imagine a more isolating set of circumstances.

Third, the presence of the Farmer provides an ongoing, if tacit, commentary on the events that will take place on his property. As Batya Casper Laks has written, this is "the first time in Western tragedy aristocracy is wedded to poverty and the peasant assumes a personality far more stable and honorable than that of the fallen artistocrat: Though humble, this man is generous, level headed and loyal." (Laks, 45)

His willingness to leave his wife "untouched," motivated by his awareness of his low status relative to hers, provides a model of noble sentiment residing in the heart of a common man. After all, social conventions would have made him perfectly "justified" in claiming his marital privileges, but he chooses to follow a higher law within himself. The murders that Electra and Orestes plan and commit will require a great deal of self–will, but of a far different character—the will to act, versus the will to refrain from acting. In the character of the Farmer, Euripides forcibly reminds us of the ever–present choice Electra and Orestes have, and refuse—to end the cycle of blood vengeance with an act of restraint rather than revenge.

Finally, the rural setting is a reminder of the natural cycles of life and death which will stand in sharp contrast to the willful taking–of–life that will occur later. The peasant women are a vivid example of this, entering breathless with anticipation as they invite Electra to join them in a marriage-blessing rite. Theirs is an invitation to life and its joys, but Electra cannot accept it. Her heart is too full of death and grief. It cannot grow lighter until she is able to discharge herself from her heart's overwhelming desire for revenge.

In Aeschylus' treatment of the tale, Orestes is the agent of this revenge. In Euripides' version, Electra takes a far more central role. Though his opening words remind us that Orestes is on a divinely sanctioned mission of revenge—coming from Apollo's oracle at Delphi, he is here "to exchange murder for my father's murder"—the role of the god, too, will take a backseat to the subsequent action of the play. Although Orestes does not explicitly include Clytemnestra in his plans, and later will struggle with himself over murdering her too, the audience would have known that matricide will indeed take place in this new setting, and will perhaps begin to glimpse here that Orestes will not act alone.

Study Questions

1. Who was Agamemnon?

2. How did Agamemnon die, according to the Farmer?

3. Why does the Farmer call a fool anyone who calls him foolish for not sleeping with his wife?

4. What has Aigisthos ordered to protect his own place on the throne?

5. Which god has charged Orestes with avenging his father's murder?

6. What has Orestes left at the tomb of Agamemnon?

7. What is Pylades' relationship to Orestes?

8. When he first sees her, who does Orestes think Electra is, and why?

9. Why are the Chorus women so happy?

10. Whom does Electra seem to blame more for her woes—her mother Clytemnestra or her mother's lover, Aigisthos?

Answers

1. Agamemnon was the victorious leader of the Greeks against Troy, husband to Clytemnestra and father to Electra and Orestes.

2. Agamemnon was killed by his wife's treachery, and the hand of Aigisthos. Aigisthos was a particularly vile rival, given that he was the son of Agamemnon's father's greatest enemy, his brother Thyestes.

3. Because of his low–born state, he considers it would be an outrage to seduce a noble woman, and argues for the virtue of self–control.

4. He has offered a bounty for the capture of Orestes and forced Electra's marriage to the Farmer to prevent her from having children with a legitimate claim to the throne.

5. Apollo has ordered the murder of his father's betrayers.

6. Orestes left a lock of his hair and a sacrificial lamb at the tomb of his father.

7. Orestes refers to Pylades as his most loyal friend.

8. Orestes sees Electra coming back from the spring, carrying a water jug, and dressed in rags, and assumes she is a farm slave.

9. The Chorus women are planning to participate in the festal rites of the goddess Hera, Zeus' wife, to ask for marriage blessings.

10. Although she targets both in her laments, more lines are devoted to her mother's treachery.

Suggested Essay Topics

1. Examine the speeches of the character of the Farmer, both in his prologue to the audience and his words to Electra, his wife. What clues to his character do we find there? How does he speak of his wife, and to her? Why might Euripides have chosen to portray this humble figure, new to a legend concerning the troubles of a royal house?

2. Given what we know so far of Electra's character, do you think Euripides intended our initial impressions to be favorable or unsympathetic? What is her grief based on, and is it meant to seem excessive or realistic? Compare what she says of her mother's actions to what the Farmer says about her, which seems in some small degree to present a different view. Whom are we meant to believe at this stage of the drama? If you believe Euripides was initially engaging our sympathy with Electra, how might you account for her response to the Chorus and Farmer, who are trying to cheer her up, and the Farmer's apparent willingness to consider Clytemnestra's side of the story?

Electra
First Episode: Electra, Orestes and Farmer

Summary

Orestes introduces himself to Electra as having news of her brother, telling her that he is alive and desires to know how his sister is faring. Electra responds by pointing to her ragged appearances and the poverty in which she lives, married to a man far beneath her station. In a long *stychomythia*, Orestes questions his sister about the reasons for this, learning of Aigisthos' fears and Electra's attempts to foil his plans by keeping her virginity secret, in the hopes that her brother will appear to help her kill both her mother and her lover.

At Orestes' invitation, Electra enumerates the humiliations she's been made to suffer. These include not only the material degradations of her new life, made more acute by the knowledge that her mother lives in luxury at the palace, but also the fact that she had to give up marriage to Castor, one of Zeus' sons and now a god. She also speaks bitterly of the exultation of Aigisthos over her father's death. He now enjoys Agamemnon's wealth, dances on his grave, and drunkenly desecrates it.

The Farmer enters, is assured that the strangers are friends, and invites them in to his home. Upon meeting him, Orestes is surprised to find "fine conscience in a poor man's frame." He meditates on the difficulty of measuring a man's worth by his wealth or appearance, and calls the Farmer a "natural aristocrat."

As Orestes enters the farmhouse, Electra berates her husband for his invitation, as they have nothing to offer these guests who outrank him. Impatiently, she sends him off in search of the old man who raised her father, so that he might bring appropriate food and drink. Arguing to himself that a man can only eat so much, and they have enough to feed their guests at least one meal, the Farmer nevertheless complies.

The Chorus ends the episode with a long account of the heroic deeds of the Greeks at Troy, led by Agamemnon, and a chilling

accusation against Clytemnestra in his murder. They, like Electra, want to see her "throat beneath the knife."

Analysis

If the original audience had been surprised by the introduction of the humble Farmer to the famous legend, in this scene they would have glimpsed more of the poet's intent in his creation. Already we have seen that Electra herself is grateful for his protection, and in his own words the Farmer has revealed himself to be a cut above the expectations of his station. But it is in Orestes' longest speech in this section that we see most clearly Euripides' mind at work.

Astonished that this humble man is willing to let his marriage go unconsummated, Orestes meditates at length on the unrecognized virtues of the common man, contrasting this example with other more noble "types" that typically merit admiration—sons of noble men, wealthy men, soldiers, men of rank in society:

> Witness this man, not great among his countrymen,
> not puffed up by his family's rank. He's one of the crowd,
> but I find him a natural aristocrat.
> Isn't it senseless to be led astray
> by preconceived notions and not judge good breeding
> by a man's company and his manners? (35)

This speech is more than a vehicle for the playwright's views on the problems of external appearance versus internal worth. Coming as it does after Electra's long speech detailing her humiliations, it also provides us with a certain lens through which to view her complaints.

When Orestes asks to know how his sister is living, Electra points first to the signs of her grief and degradation: her wasted frame, her ugly hair, a marriage she equates with death. But we remember that her husband has not required heavy labor, and from the Chorus we know that Electra has been mourning beyond the reasonable period and actually has access through them to better clothes. We might begin to suspect here that Electra is too tied to the world of appearances, fearing that unless she looks the part, her feelings won't be taken seriously—a position which Orestes in-

indirectly argues against in his speech.

Later, in enumerating the wrongs she's suffered, Electra continually contrasts her high–born origins with her new lowly state. The "daughter of a royal house," she now mucks around in filth, dressed in "robes fit for a cowshed." She, who was once promised to be wed to a god, now has to forsake the company of other girls, because she is married, and the dances of other wives, because she has remained a virgin. Meanwhile, she torments herself by thinking of all the luxuries her mother continues to enjoy at the palace. She even envies her mother's slaves. Her description of Aigisthos' sacrilegious behavior stands in sharp contrast to an account of him delivered by a messenger later in the play.

The entrance of the Farmer at the end of this speech, which motivates Orestes' musings, provides a subtle comment on the shallowness of Electra's complaint. For she barely mentions her father in this grief. Her fury is reserved for herself and her "unbearable" state, and seems to be based more on the loss of material comforts than the loss of her father. The presence of the Farmer, then, stands as a mute refutation of her miseries, given voice later in Orestes' speech. It is left to the audience to draw this connection. In her humble state, Electra might have chosen to display the nobility she claims is her birthright by acting more as the Farmer does. Instead, she consistently draws attention to her squalor, and even in the face of Orestes' admiration of him, proceeds to scold her husband for his lack of breeding in showing hospitality to his "superior" guests.

The effect of this is to help us question the motives of the character whose name lends the play its title. If Clytemnestra is indeed deserving of her known fate, what does it mean that it is achieved through the efforts of an Electra who is starting to seem more self–interested than self–justified? This question will pervade the rest of the play.

Study Questions

1. How does Orestes present himself to Electra?
2. When Orestes asks what he should do "if" he comes home, what does Electra respond?

3. Why does Electra not recognize her brother?

4. Who is the only man whom Electra claims would recognize him?

5. What does Electra claim she would do to "let blood from her mother's throat?"

6. Why does Electra envy her mother's slaves?

7. What is Electra's accusation against Agamemnon, besides the fact that he participated in her father's murder?

8. What is the Farmer's response to meeting the two travelers?

9. After he has met the Farmer and learned of his gentle decency, what does Orestes concludes matters more than appearance?

10. To which Greek hero of the Trojan War does the Chorus sing an ode to at the end of this episode?

Answers

1. Orestes claims he is a friend of "himself," come to bring the news that he is still alive, though drifting from place to place.

2. Electra claims he must act against his father's killers, both of them, and with the same axe they used on him.

3. The pair were separated when they were young.

4. Electra says the only man who could recognize Orestes is the old tutor who helped to raise her father—the same man she sends the Farmer off to bring back with food and drink.

5. Electra claims she would die to do this.

6. She says they wear clothes of fine wool, fastened by gold, while she has to wear rags.

7. She claims he's taken advantage of her father's position, and left his grave unattended, except to desecrate it with drunken oaths and mockery against Orestes.

8. At first he is suspicious, claiming it is not seemly for young women to be seen in the company of men. When he learns

they are friends of Orestes, however, he welcomes them into
his house.

9. Orestes says that only character and courage matter, not the
    mere appearance of them.

10. They sing the praises of Achilles.

Suggested Essay Topics

1. If at first we might be inclined to sympathize with Electra's
    plight, in this episode we see perhaps a different interpreta-
    tion emerging. How does Euripides begin this transforma-
    tion? Compare her speeches with those of the Farmer and
    Orestes in this scene. How does what they say tend to present
    what she says in a different light?

2. Like Aeschylus before him, Euripides chose to have the sib-
    lings not immediately recognize each other, and in having
    Orestes withhold his true identity from Electra after he knows
    who she is. What dramatic purpose is served by this choice?
    How does this affect the presentation of Electra's character?
    You may want to refer also to earlier discussions in the *Medea*
    section on dramatic irony.

Electra
Second Episode: Electra, Orestes, and the Old Man

New Character:

Old Man: *former tutor of Agamemnon, living on the outskirts of
Argos*

Summary

The Old Man arrives, carrying with him a lamb, flowers,
cheeses, and wine. He is crying because on his way he has stopped
to pay tribute at the tomb of Agamemnon, whom he helped to raise.

He noticed the relics left there (by Orestes), and wonders who would have been brave enough to honor Aigisthos' enemy, and suggests it may have been Orestes himself.

To test his theory, he holds the lock of hair he found there up to Electra's shorn head, to see if it matches. Though it does, Electra does not take him seriously, arguing that it is no proof of shared blood. She further refutes two other arguments offered by the Old Man in support of his belief, and she concludes that the offerings were left by strangers.

The Old Man asks to see her guests. When he meets them he cautions himself not to take their well–born appearance as proof of anything. He begins closely to scrutinize Orestes, examining him from every angle. Finally he exclaims that, because of a peculiar scar on Orestes' forehead, there can be no doubt of his identity. Brother and sister embrace, and the Chorus sings a hymn of joy.

When Orestes asks the Old Man if there are any friends left who might wish him well, the Old Man replies that although he is indeed friendless, Orestes has everything he needs within him to take back his rights—by killing both Aigisthos and Clytemnestra.

There follows a lengthy *stychomythia* in which the Old Man helps Orestes devise a plan. Aigisthos is in a nearby meadow, preparing a sacrificial feast. Orestes will travel there, get himself invited to share the feast, and make his "next play."

Clytemnestra has planned to join her husband later, to avoid the ridicule of the people. When Orestes wonders how he will kill them both, Electra replies: "I myself will arrange my mother's death." To this end, she sends the Old Man back to the palace with the false report that she has given birth to a son and desires Clytemnestra's help in conducting the postpartum rites. When her mother arrives, she will be killed. Before they depart, all three pray to the gods and to the spirits of Agamemnon and his men to protect and assist their efforts, if they believe their cause to be just.

To Orestes, Electra delivers an urgent speech, telling him that if he fails, she will kill herself. The Old Man leaves with Orestes and Pylades to show them the way to Aigisthos' meadow, and then on to deliver Electra's message to Clytemnestra. Electra goes inside to await news of the outcome of Orestes' task.

The Chorus passes the time with a retelling of a legend about the house of Atreus. Agamemnon's father, Atreus, had been given the gift of a golden ram by Pan, as proof of his kingship of Argos. His brother Thyestes was jealous, and lured Atreus' wife away from him and stole the ram. This, in turn, provoked Zeus to change the course of the heavens, turning earth into a vast desert. All of men's misfortunes since then were caused by Thyestes' crime. Their ode closes with a reminder to Clytemnestra that she too has provoked the wrath of the gods by murdering her husband.

Analysis

In this famous "recognition scene," most scholars agree that Euripides is poking fun at Aeschylus' treatment of the various signs of Orestes' identity, that, in the earlier play, Electra dared not hope were true. In this one, she refutes them one by one and in no uncertain terms. To the lock of hair, she replies that anyone can share the same hair type. This is not proof of blood relation. When the Old Man then points to the footprints on the path, asking that she step in them to see if they too match, Electra replies that even if footprints were possible on a stony path, her brother's would be much larger than her own. Finally, when the Old Man suggests Orestes might be recognized by some piece of clothing she'd woven for him in their youth, Electra responds that in the first place, she was too young to have done so, and in the second, he would have outgrown it by now.

Considering that the audience would have been quite familiar with the Aeschylean treatment of this scene, many scholars have found that it very nearly degenerates into parody. What rescues it, if barely, is the final sign which even Electra in her obstinance cannot refute—the scar on Orestes' forehead, which was impossible to outgrow and more firmly binding than any external sign. Euripides may be using the scar as a symbol to subtly reinforce the idea that external appearances count for less than inherent characteristics, though some argue the scar was too convenient and wonder why it took Electra so long to recognize it.

Philip Velacott has suggested that this scene serves another dramatic purpose, by highlighting the reluctance of both siblings to recognize each other. This recognition is delayed, he argues, because neither of them wants fully to face the inevitable conse-

quences of their reunion. Electra will be forced to give up the grievances she has nursed for so long, and Orestes will be forced to
murderous action.

If the audience has enjoyed this interlude of comic relief, however, it is rather short–lived, as soon the pair get down to the business of planning the revenge. Orestes is dispatched to virtually
ambush Aigisthos at his outdoor feast. For her part, Electra has assumed responsibility for luring her mother to her home.

This last is a curious twist in the ongoing indirect characterization of Clytemnestra. We have heard Electra's ravings about her
mother's scheming, her idle pursuit of luxury in an adulterer's bed;
and it seems to matter little to Electra that it was through
Clytemnestra's intervention that she was married off rather than
killed outright. Yet she knows her mother will come to her side,
claiming that she will be hurt by the recognition of her "son's" low
birth. Like the Old Man, we are left wondering if Clytemnestra is
so evil, why should she concern herself further with her banished
daughter? Electra's answer seems unsatisfying, and we can only
wonder if in fact the playwright was showing us that the truth and
Electra's perception of it might in fact be two quite different things.

The answer, as in all things Euripidean, is never quite clear.
Certainly the Old Man refers to Clytemnestra as that "ungodly
woman," and the Chorus, with Electra, assigns the blame for
Agamemnon's death to her. But if we concern ourselves with the
development of Electra's character, we can see that with almost
every speech she gives, her vision of revenge narrows itself to bring
Clytemnestra ever closer in its sights. But before Clytemnestra
herself can appear to defend herself, we must learn the outcome
of Orestes' murderous expedition.

Study Questions

1. Who is the Old Man?

2. What are the signs he points to that prove it was Orestes who
    recently visited Agamemnon's grave?

3. What is the final proof of Orestes' identity?

4. What does the Old Man tell Orestes he must do to avenge
    his father?

5. What part will Orestes play in the plan?

6. What is Electra's role?

7. Who are the pair's allies in this plan?

8. To whom and for what do the trio pray before Orestes sets off?

9. According to the Chorus, what caused Zeus to reverse the course of the sun and send famine to the earth?

10. To what is this long–ago crime compared?

Answers

1. He was the tutor of Agamemnon, who helped Orestes to escape being killed by Aigisthos.

2. The Old Man suggests that the lock of hair left at the grave, a set of footprints leading from it, and a piece of cloth woven for him by Electra before they were separated would prove Orestes' identity.

3. Orestes has a scar on his forehead, which he got while chasing after a fawn with Electra in their childhood.

4. The Old Man says he must kill both Aigisthos and Clytemnestra.

5. Orestes will endeavor to meet Aigisthos in a nearby meadow, where the latter has come to prepare a sacrificial feast. Orestes is to murder him there.

6. She will lure her mother to her home, on the pretext that she needs her help in performing the post–partum rights over her fictional newborn son.

7. The Old Man delivers her message to Clytemnestra and shows Orestes the way to Aigisthos' feast; and Pylades, though mute throughout, accompanies Orestes on his mission.

8. Orestes, the Old Man and Electra pray to Zeus, to Hera, to the Earth, to the spirit of their slain father, and to all the men of Greece who died under his command to protect and aid them in their quest.

9. The Chorus recounts the legend that Agamemnon's uncle's treachery, in stealing both his mother and the sign of his father's kingship, was a mortal crime that provoked the wrath of the gods.

10. The Chorus compares it to Clytemnestra's crime in slaying her husband.

Suggested Essay Topics

1. Comment on the role of the Chorus thus far in the play. What is their relationship to Electra, and how do they manifest this in their dealings with her? Are they as important so far in the play as the *Medea* Chorus was? Reviewing the various functions of the Chorus as outlined in the introduction to this study guide, do you think the Chorus is essential in providing the audience with a guideline for how to assess the actions of the other characters, or do you find that in this case they seem more important for reinforcing various characterizations, particularly of Electra and Clytemnestra? Support your views with examples from the Choral passages.

2. Suppose for a moment that Euripides' was the first dramatic treatment of the Electra legend, and the recognition scene was completely his invention. In your estimation, what does it add to or detract from the play in terms of character development, dramatic pacing, and the emotional tone of the eventual recognition itself? Do you think the play would still need this scene, or would it benefit from its being cut?

Electra
Third Episode: The Messenger and Orestes' Return

New Character:

Messenger: *one of Orestes' servants*

Summary

From offstage are heard the "howls of death," and one of Orestes' servants finally arrives to tell what happened at the site of Aigisthos' feast. The news is good. Orestes has succeeded.

Electra presses him for details, and learns how Aigisthos, believing that Orestes was from Thessaly as he claimed, invited him and his party to join his feast. While Aigisthos was praying to the Nymphs for continued prosperity for himself and his wife, and victory over their enemies, Orestes proceeded to butcher Aigisthos' sacrificial calf. In its entrails Aigisthos read a dire prophesy that Agamemnon's son was stalking him. As Aigisthos leaned forward to inspect the heart and lungs, Orestes took up the cleaver and plunged it into Aigisthos' backbone.

It was a difficult death, and when it was over, the servants raised their spears to battle Orestes and Pylades. But Orestes convinced them he meant no one else harm, and once they recognized him they crowned him in support. The Messenger reports that even now he is on his way, bearing the head of Aigisthos.

The Chorus and Electra rejoice at this news. Electra goes off in search of a wreath to crown the head of her victorious brother, while the Chorus anticipates a new rule by a just king who has himself "killed injustice."

Orestes and company return, bearing the body of the murdered Aigisthos, whose head he presents to Electra. At first reluctant to speak ill of the dead, Electra proceeds to "catalogue his wrongs" to Aigisthos' dead face. Beginning with Agamemnon's murder, she goes on to taunt him for his tainted character, his marrying into wealth, his allowing Clytemnestra to control him, and his preening vanity. Her only regret is that he could not have survived to see how just a price he has at last paid.

Electra sends the Chorus off to hide Aegisthos' body, so that her mother won't see it when she arrives. At this point, Orestes begins to have second thoughts about killing their mother. As he waivers, Electra reminds him that "If even Apollo's judgment fails, is anyone wise?" She says that their father has not yet been fully avenged. Orestes even begins to doubt the truth of Apollo's orders, and it is not until Electra makes an appeal to his manhood that he

at last re–commits himself. He exits into the farmhouse, calling his "sport" "bitter," to await his mother's arrival.

Analysis

In this episode Euripides begins to flesh out the character of the victims, and in so doing, the character of his protagonists as well. Through the messenger's words, we meet Aigisthos, not as the drunken cavorter over the grave of his enemy, but as a man engaged in the peaceful pursuit of gathering myrtle for his hair in a "stream–watered garden." When he meets Orestes and his followers, he greets them warmly, and when told they are Thessalians on their way to Zeus' shrine, he invites them to pass the night with him at his feast. His invitation is sincere. He "takes our hands/tugging us forward. 'You must not say No.'" He never suspects he has welcomed his own murderer into his company until it is too late. Orestes ambushes him from behind as he leans over to learn more of what the butchered calf's entrails have to say.

Here the picture of Aigisthos is far different from the one painted by Electra in the earlier scenes. He is presented as a warm and generous host, taken from behind almost while he is in the act of prayer. Despite the fact of Aigisthos' known collaboration in Agamemnon's death, he seems to have mellowed in the intervening years, and bears little resemblance to the disgusting creature depicted by Electra earlier and again in her address to his lifeless head. What is Euripides purpose here?

This scene is perhaps best understood as another example of Euripides bringing the heroic figures of Electra and Orestes, as portrayed by Aeschylus and Sophocles, into the realm of everyday mortals. The Messenger's description provides another mirror reflecting Aigisthos, held against Electra's description. Whose vision is distorted, and whose is true? It seems that the Messenger has little to gain by misrepresenting Aigisthos, so his characterization of him seems included by Euripides in order to cast further suspicion on Electra's fevered imagination.

For example, when invited to speak her mind to the dead Aigisthos, she abandons all reliance on convention and proceeds to indulge herself in a frenzy of insults. She goes so far as to suggest that while she was at the palace he strutted in front of her as though he was considering marrying her himself.

> ...I'll merely hint at what I know.
> How you strutted and preened, living in a king's house,
> showing off your well–made body. But I want no
> girl–faced husband....(56)

We know from the Farmer that Aigisthos' designs were on Electra's life, not her hand. And further, we know from the legend that she is a daughter of a woman who killed her husband. Given everything Electra holds against him, why would he ever consider marrying her? If Electra's delusions are part of Euripides' plan to show the tragic consequences of the wrongs done her, they nevertheless also provide a portrait of a self–absorbed, vain young woman with whom it is difficult to identify.

Neither does Orestes escape criticism from Euripides' pen, as revealed in two key passages. One tells of his refusal to bathe before Aigisthos' feast, and the other reveals the manner of Aigisthos' murder. The invitation to bathe was a convention extended to all guests at a ritual banquet, to prevent them from contaminating the offerings. By lying to Aigisthos, Orestes shows that he is aware that to participate fully in the banquet would be to commit not only an act of revenge, but a sacrilege as well. It may be argued that this is evidence of Orestes' conscience at work. But in his later unsportsmanlike murder we have reason to suspect that his conscience is not over–active.

His final words to Aigisthos, before he drives the cleaver into his back, brim with irony, as he reassures him that the prophesy of the calf's entrails could not apply to him. Then, without giving Aigisthos the chance to meet his enemy face to face, he cowardly stabs him in the back. So much for the brave avenger, whom Electra crowns with "a wreath that could grace a god's head." If she and the Chorus cannot see Orestes' failings, the audience surely can. Yet, at the same time, we should remember, there was a price on Orestes' head. But does that in any way mitigate his methods?

Orestes' waivering on the verge of killing his mother may speak more to his filial feelings than his cowardly ones. However, in the face of his vacillation Electra only grows more inhuman. Demanding that he "let no coward's thoughts topple [his] manhood," she tries to instill in him the same "guile" their mother used to murder her own husband.

Despite this comparison if Electra never sees how truly similar those acts are, if she cannot explain how Orestes' act of revenge will somehow make him immune to retribution himself, the audience might think otherwise. We might also ask ourselves, is not her desire somehow understandable, given all she's been made to suffer? In Euripides' hands, these two views remain in constant tension with each other, making for a gripping drama and an unforgettable character.

Study Questions

1. What is Electra prepared to do when she first hears the off-stage "howls of death"?

2. What is her response to the Messenger when she first sees him?

3. What is the lie Orestes told Aigisthos to mask his identity?

4. For whom was Aigisthos preparing his feast?

5. Why did Orestes butcher the calf?

6. Why is Orestes given the cleaver with which he will kill Aigisthos?

7. Who among Aigisthos' company recognized Orestes?

8. Why does Electra's long speech to Aigisthos' corpse stand against convention?

9. Why does Electra think Aigisthos is a military coward?

10. What does Orestes' say about Apollo's prophesy when faced with the idea of killing his own mother?

Answers

1. Electra is prepared to plunge the sword into her own heart if they prove Orestes has been bested.

2. She is suspicious, and demands he make him believe her.

3. Orestes tells Aigisthos that he and his company are from Thessaly, on their way to a shrine to Zeus.

4. Aigisthos was sacrificing a calf to the Nymphs.

5. He butchered the calf at Aigisthos' flattering invitation, to prove the reputation of "Thessalians" at such tasks.

6. He claims he is going to use it to break the rib cage of the calf.

7. Orestes is recognized by an old man who had been at court before Orestes was banished.

8. It was considered shameful to speak ill of the dead.

9. She reminds him (or his corpse) that while her father led the Greeks in Troy, Aigisthos himself "shirked the war."

10. Orestes claims,"I'll never believe the prophesy rings true."

Suggested Essay Topics

1. Do you agree that the Messenger's speech serves to illustrate the difference between Electra's perceptions and reality? If so, what is Euripides' point in making this illustration? If not, how might you account for the two different views of Aigisthos that are presented?

2. In Electra's speech over Aigisthos' body, she devotes only three lines to his murder of her father, and the rest to an assassination of his character. Analyze this speech in terms of the "catalogue" of her complaints. How are her arguments structured? Do they proceed logically, or jump from point to point? Are they based in information we have received from other sources, or are some of them seeming creations in her mind? What are some of the images she uses to describe him? How does the speech work to reveal the state of her emotions at this point in the play?

Electra
Fourth Episode: Electra, Clytemnestra, and Orestes

New Character:

Clytemnestra: *mother of Orestes and Electra; unknowing widow of Aigisthos*

Summary

Clytemnestra arrives in all her royal finery, accompanied by an entourage of Trojan women slaves. The Chorus greets her with respect, but Electra wastes little time in accusing her mother of casting her out from her home. To this Clytemnestra replies that she faults Agamemnon, who lured their daughter Iphigenia to her death at Aulis and then came home with another mistress. In clear words, she admits she killed him, and asks Electra what Agamemnon's actions would have been if, under similar circumstances, she had killed Orestes. Believing that a killer should be executed, she took the only path open to her—joining her husband's enemies to bring him down.

The Chorus responds by conceding that the reasons for the murder are just, but the means in this case are "ugly." A woman should defer in all things to her husband in order to be considered a proper wife. Electra, for her part, begins another "catalogue" of faults, starting with Clytemnestra's vanity over her appearance after her husband had left for Troy. Electra takes this to be the behavior of a wanton woman. She accuses her mother of being the only Greek to desire Troy's victory, because she hoped that her husband would not return home. Finally, Electra asks why, if Clytemnestra's complaint was with her former husband, has she made her other children to suffer as they have? Electra concludes with a vow that she and Orestes will kill her.

Clytemnestra excuses Electra's outburst, explaining it as the result of her daughter's stronger affection for Agamemnon, and admitting that she has no cause to rejoice in her own actions.

Electra persists until Clytemnestra finally asks her why she's asked her to come. Upon hearing Electra's false tale of her newborn son, and seeing the circumstance in which she lives, Clytemnestra agrees to help with the rituals. Electra follows her into the farmhouse, whispering of the knife that awaits her there. The Chorus rehearses once more Agamemnon's murder, for the first time characterizing it as "just payment."

Clytemnestra's cries are heard from within the house, as she begs her children not to kill her. Electra, Pylades and Orestes, spattered with blood, bring the bodies of Clytemnestra and Aigisthos out of the farmhouse. Orestes and Electra show remorse for what they've done, as they describe their actions. Orestes had to cover his eyes with his cloak as Electra took his hand and guided the knife home. "Of most dreadful suffering," she says, "I am the cause." They cover Clytemnestra's body with robes and hope that here the sufferings of their house will end.

Analysis

In this climactic scene, Clytemnestra has a brief say before her fate is sealed in her daughter's farmhouse. As with the treatment of Aigisthos in the previous scene, she is not presented as the unremittingly evil monster of her daughter's imagination. If she were, it would be easy for us to cheer her children on. As it is, we can only shake our heads with the Chorus as they remark: "No family and its many generations/have been more their own victim."

Clytemnestra's representation of how Agamemnon betrayed and murdered their daughter, then compounded her humiliation by bringing home a new mistress, is calculated to temper Electra's hate, and also to win the audience's sympathy for her. In this debate it's interesting to note, as D.J. Conacher has pointed out, that mother and daughter resemble each other to some extent. Both tend to hurry past the relevant facts of the matter to dwell more on the issues of jealousy they raise. As Electra glossed over Agamemnon's murder in her address to Aigisthos' corpse, so Clytemnestra devotes more time to Agamemnon's adultery and her sister Helen's lust for Paris than she does to the initial sacrifice she claims motivated her own act of revenge.

But she admits to this act, and permits her daughter to call it

unjust. Here Electra responds not so much to the murder motivating her own desire for revenge, as to her mother's character, which she labels as sluttish. Why else would she have spent long hours at the mirror, making herself pretty while her husband was away? More to the point, why, if concern for her lost daughter was so central to her argument, did she consign her other two children to the living deaths of exile?

Although she has invited Electra's rebuttal, Clytemnestra seems almost too tired to argue it, acknowledging only that Electra had always preferred her father to her. She adds that she too has not found "much reason in [her] own acts for rejoicing." Never acknowledging Electra's clear threat, she tries to change the subject to the reason for her visit, not suspecting for a moment what it really is. This, in turn, provides Electra with another opportunity to blame her mother for her reduced circumstances, as she sarcastically invites her into her "humble house" and reminds her not to ruin her finery by brushing up against its soot.

The Chorus here provides a sort of barometer for the mixed feelings the audience must, by now, be experiencing, as they recount both Agamemnon's and Clytemnestra's crimes. Hearing the screams within the farmhouse, they can only lament: "Savage your death, poor creature, but godless the death you devised." (65)

More than the other two classic playwrights who treated the theme, Euripides dwells on the after-effects of the matricide. The remainder of the scene is devoted to an exploration of the remorse the brother and sister feel, though in Electra's case she never goes so far as to admit she wishes they hadn't done the deed. Orestes' first words are to call his actions "poor reparation" for the wrongs he's suffered, and Electra emerges with tears of guilt and shame.

Now Orestes is able to see the paradox in the god's directive. If its wisdom was hidden, its torment is now clear. He cannot shake the images of his mother's pleas for mercy, and he feels compelled to repeat them in graphic detail to the Chorus. Electra is facing up to the consequences of the act that was supposed to set her free.

> And where, oh where shall I go? What dancing be mine?
> What marriage? What husband will lead me,
> a bride, to his bed? (66)

To this the Chorus replies that it's too late to think of such things now, after she's already bent her brother's mind to act against its own will!

Whether because of their words or her own change of heart, Electra takes full responsibility for the act, and, gently draping a cloak around her mother's body, hopes for "an end of great woe for our house."

On the surface, Orestes' and Electra's reactions may seem only natural, if tragically delayed. But Philip Velacott has suggested that there is more at stake, and in this scene we see Euripides' desire to further question the wisdom of the gods in directing the moral life of human beings. Unable to trust their own moral instincts, the pair have relied on Apollo's sanctions to justify their actions—a view supported by both Aeschylus and Sophocles in their treatments of the myth. In Euripides' hands, says Velacott, Electra and Orestes, "being weak, preferred sin under authority to the risks of moral independence." In this scene, the consequences of that weakness are given full play.

Batya Casper Laks offers another provocative answer to the question of why Euripides chose to dwell on the change of heart at such length. In Laks' view, Orestes' and Electra's destruction of the mother, and their subsequent awakening to the remorse this causes, is a dramatic symbol of the psychological journey out of adolescence and into mature reality. In this journey, the human conscience learns how to hold two contradictory emotions at once: "Avenging him, I am pure; but killing her, condemned." (Laks, 49) In this play, according to Laks, the modern hero first emerges, and marks a significant departure from the more uni–dimensional heroes of classic Greek tragedy.

Study Questions

1. According to the Chorus, who are Clytemnestra's brothers, and what have they become?

2. To what other sibling of Clytemnestra does Electra refer?

3. Which double standard does Clytemnestra complain of in her defense to Electra?

4. Why does Clytemnestra feel Iphigenia's death so bitterly?

5. What is Electra's interpretation of the sacrifice of her sister, relative to Clytemnestra's response to it?

6. How does Electra compare her situation to her sister's?

7. After the matricide, what are Orestes' and Electra's fears for the future?

8. How did Clytemnestra try to stop Orestes from killing her?

9. How was Orestes able to complete the act?

10. Who does Electra say is ultimately responsible for the matricide, and why?

Answers

1. The Chorus greets her as "sister of Zeus' sons, Castor and Polydeukes," who are now the patron gods of sailors.

2. Electra unfavorably compares Clytemnestra to her sister Helen, for whom the Trojan War was fought.

3. Clytemnestra claims that when women stray from marriage they are strongly censured, but when men do, they "hear no reproach."

4. She claims that Iphigenia was sacrificed only because Menelaos could not control his wife Helen's lust, and therefore started a senseless war. If the cause was just and his own city or family threatened, Agamemnon's act would have been excusable.

5. Electra believes it was just an excuse on Clytemnestra's part to kill her husband, because she was thinking of other men as soon as he left for the war.

6. Electra claims hers is a "living death," worse than her sister's quick death.

7. Orestes fears perpetual exile, for no country will welcome a man who killed his own mother; while Electra feels no man would have her for the same reason.

8. According to Orestes, she tried to provoke his pity by cupping his face in her hands, and calling him, "My son, my own son."

9. Orestes could only kill his mother by first covering his eyes with his cloak; Electra had to guide his hands, participating herself with open eyes.

10. Electra asserts that because she "called the stroke" and guided the knife home, she is the cause of her mother's death.

Suggested Essay Topics

1. Compare the speeches in the "debate" between mother and daughter in this scene. In what ways do they resemble each other, and in what ways are they different? Comment both on the content and the emotional tone of the speeches, with reference to such stylistic devices as imagery, simile and metaphor.

2. Compare the picture of Orestes that has emerged by the end of this episode with the one painted by Electra at the beginning of the play. From Electra's speeches, what kind of man might we expect him to be? As we follow Orestes' own words and actions, do we find that he consistently lives up to this expectation, or do certain cracks in his character appear? Provide supporting examples from various moments in the play.

Electra
Final Episode and Exodos

New Characters:

Castor and Polydeukes: *twin demi–gods, sons of Zeus and half–brothers of Clytemnestra*

Summary

The Dioskouroi, Castor and Polydeukes, appear as shining stars on the roof of the farmhouse, and announce they have come on Zeus' orders to pronounce a sort of sentence on Orestes and Electra for their "unjust act." Electra is to marry Pylades, forfeiting her inheritance and leaving Argos forever. Her Farmer husband is to accompany them, and Pylades to reward him handsomely for his kindness.

Orestes, too, is bound to exile, but first he must travel to Athens to stand trial for the murder. There, the demi–gods predict, the goddess Pallas Athena will protect Orestes from the Furies, the snake–like goddesses of doom who will pursue him. At the trial, Apollo will assume the guilt for the matricide, and a new law will be established that if a verdict is evenly split, the accused will go free. The goddesses of doom will be forever thwarted, and Orestes will live out his days in the wilds of Arkadia.

Aigisthos and Clytemnestra are to be given honorable burials. As for Helen, the gods reveal that she "never went to Troy" at all; rather, her image only was used by Zeus in his own desire to provoke war among men.

Electra asks the gods why they did nothing to protect their sister Clytemnestra, to which Castor replies that they could not overrule Apollo's decree. Then Electra asks what that decree had to do with *her* killing her mother, but Castor avoids the question, instead recalling the curse that destined both her father and mother to die.

Tearfully, Orestes and Electra take leave of each other forever. Electra leaves with Pylades, and Orestes runs off, pursued by the goddesses of doom. Castor and Polydeukes have business to attend to elsewhere, but before they leave they caution humans to "hold precious in life all things godly and just," for they will find no rescue if they don't. The Chorus expresses a desire for a life blessed by joy before they too make their slow exit, and the play ends.

Analysis

As the Chorus makes its brief and feeble plea for joy in the final moment of the play, we are left with the feelings of ambivalence that Euripides so excelled at provoking. We feel neither the relief at knowing that moral order has been definitively restored, nor are we able to fully condemn this matricidal pair, who are now forced to live out their lives exiled in a morally ambiguous world. Instead, we may achieve some degree of pity for these characters, whose truest friendship resides almost solely in each other, and who are forced nevertheless to separate forever.

If Aeschylus and Sophocles presented Orestes and Electra as heroes on a grand scale whose actions, though tragic, were nevertheless divinely ordered, Euripides is unwilling at his play's end to offer such security. The appearance of gods at the end of a play was not uncommon in ancient tragedy, particularly in the work of Euripides. It is a dramatic device usually referred to as the *"deus ex machina"* (god out of the machine). Such an appearance usually signified a return to order in which human actions are made to conform to divine wisdom.

In the words of Castor, however, we are invited to question that divine sanction.

> Apollo, Apollo—but he is my lord. I will
> keep silence. He is wise forever, though his oracle
> spoke brutal words. We are bound to acquiesce. (68)

It is as though Castor wishes he could say more in direct critique, but in the hierarchy of Olympus he is forced to defer judgment to his higher master. Later he is more direct when he says, "Fate and the unwise cry of Apollo fulfilled necessity's binding command". (69)

This last is in response to Electra's challenge that the Dioskouroi could have helped prevent their sister's tragic end. When in the next few lines she further challenges the gods to explain when Apollo ever ordained that she herself should kill her mother, Castor neatly sidesteps the issue to invoke a more common tragic dictate of fate. To Electra's ultimately unanswerable questions the gods can provide no consoling answers. Even the Trojan War is blamed on Zeus, and meaningful resolution to the human condition in the face of such divine inconstancy seems far away.

As though to confirm this, Castor closes with a warning to mortals that it is up to us to "hold precious in life all things/godly and just." The suggestion is that the gods are not necessarily reliable aids in this endeavor.

If throughout the play Euripides alternately invited and resisted our sympathetic response to Electra and Orestes, by the end he seems to have invited our compassion, if not our complete identification with these characters. Their suffering is far from over. Neither can reclaim the heritage they thought would be restored by their actions; nor can they return to their ancestral home. They must endure separation from each other to make their way in a hostile world. Though the cycle of blood vengeance ends with them and they escape the retribution such a cycle would demand, as we noted above, the sentence of exile is just as harsh to the Greek mind.

So we may come to pity this pair, and our pity might be liberally seasoned with fear, in our own recognition that we share something of the general human condition with these troubled protagonists. For Aristotle, this combination of pity and fear was the proper and powerful aim of all great tragedies. That Euripides could have so masterfully combined these emotions in such a disturbing way is testament that his *Electra* rightfully shares an honored place among them.

Study Questions

1. Why have the Dioskouroi (Castor and Polydeukes) appeared at the farmhouse?

2. Who will protect Orestes from the hounding goddesses of doom?

3. Where will Orestes' trial take place?

4. How will the court decide on the matter of Orestes' matricide, and why?

5. Where will Orestes then live out his days?

6. What is to become of Electra?

7. What will be the fate of the Farmer, and the bodies of Clytemnestra and Aigisthos?

8. With what two questions does Electra challenge divine wisdom?

9. What does the Chorus see that makes them warn Orestes to run toward Athens?

10. Where are the Dioskouroi bound as they exit the scene?

Answers

1. Having witnessed the "sacrifice" of Clytemnestra, they are there to prophesy the fate of Electra and Orestes.

2. • Pallas Athena, the patron deity of Athens, will provide her protection.

3. Orestes will be tried in court on the hill of Ares, nearby to Athens.

4. Castor suggests that it will be an even vote, and that because Apollo will take responsibility Orestes will be acquitted.

5. Orestes will found a new city near the river of Arkadia.

6. Electra is to marry Pylades, and live with him in his city.

7. The Farmer will accompany Electra and Pylades, and be rewarded with "wealth beyond his dreams." Clytemnestra and Aigisthos are to be given decent burials in their native land.

8. She first asks why the demi–gods did not come to the aid of their sister Clytemnestra. Next she asks how Apollo's orders bear on her own guilt.

9. They see the goddesses of doom in hot pursuit of him, "black flesh and snake–hands coiling/round a fruit of agonizing pain."

10. Castor and Polydeukes, as patrons of sailors at sea, are off to protect the ships in the high seas off Sicily.

Suggested Essay Topics

1. How has Euripides worked, in this scene and the previous one, to effect a transformation of character on both Orestes and Electra? How do their words and actions in these two scenes compare with their words and actions in earlier scenes? Is Electra as tormented, Orestes as heroic as originally presented? What clues in their dialogue support your conclusions?

2. How does Euripides use the speeches of Castor to suggest
    that Electra and Orestes are now worthy of our compassion?
    Is there a clue in Castor's apparent eagerness to minimize
    the suffering that awaits them, exiled from home and from
    each other?

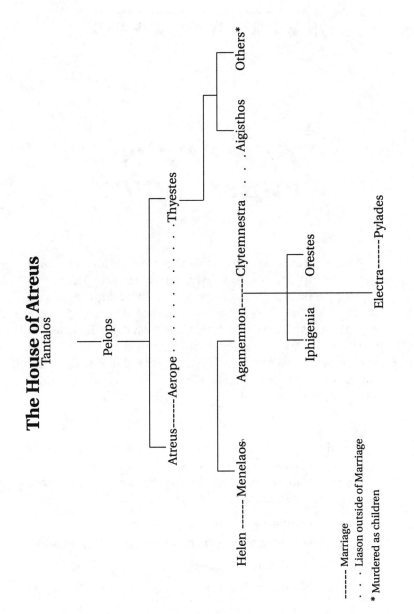

The House of Atreus
Tantalos

Pelops

Atreus------Aerope · · · · · · · · · ·Thyestes

Menelaos

Helen ------ Menelaos

Agamemnon------Clytemnestra · · · ·Aigisthos

Others*

Iphigenia

Orestes

Electra------Pylades

------ Marriage
· · · Liason outside of Marriage
* Murdered as children

SECTION FOUR

Sample Analytical Paper Topics

Topic #1

In the various legends telling the tale of Medea's revenge against her faithless husband Jason, the character of Medea was almost universally drawn as monstrous and mad, with her powers as a sorceress (or witch) almost universally foregrounded. There was little to suggest her human side. Although Euripides invented the monstrous act of infanticide for her, he was also able to show that she was a master of logical argumentation and that as a mother, this act was extremely painful to her as well. How does Euripides paint a more fully–fleshed character in his *Medea*?

Outline

I. Thesis Statement: *As drawn by Euripides, the character of Medea is neither monsterous nor mad. She is, rather, a three-dimensional woman driven by character and circumstance to commit unthinkable acts.*

II. Scenes Arguing Against Medea's "Madness"

    A. Medea's initial address to the Chorus in the first episode.

    B. Medea's debate with Creon.

    C. Medea's debate with Jason.

    D. Medea's scene with Aegeus.

    E. Medea's second scene with Jason.

    F. The Choral passage after Medea has killed her sons.

III. Scenes of Medea's Maternal Dimensions

    A. Medea's scene with Creon.

    B. Medea's second scene with Jason.

    C. Medea's self–debate in the Fifth Episode, after the children have been to the palace.

IV. Scenes Revealing the Problematic Circumstances Influencing Medea

    A. The Nurse's prologue.

    B. Medea's initial address to the Chorus.

    C. The Tutor's news that Medea and the children are to be banished, and Jason's seeming indifference to that fact.

    D. Medea's first debate with Jason.

    E. Aegeus' response to Medea's story.

    F. Medea's final episode with Jason.

    G. The ongoing response of the Chorus to Medea's plight.

V. Euripides' implied messages about the lot of women, and his critique of cold dynastic ambition as represented by Jason.

Topic #2

Appearance vs. reality is a central motif running throughout *Electra*, which Euripides uses both to develop his characters and to make a point to his audience. Discuss the ways in which this motif is played out through the course of the play.

Outline

I. Thesis Statement: *Throughout* Electra, *Euripides opposes the appearance of things to their reality, to provide subtle commentary on the title character, and to suggest that an over–reliance on external appearances can be dangerous.*

II. Appearance vs. Reality in the Character of Electra

A. The hardship of her lot as Electra perceives it, versus the willingness of the Farmer and Chorus to ease it in the first episode.

B. The characterization of Clytemnestra by Electra versus her characterization by the Farmer and by Clytemnestra herself.

C. The characterization of Aigisthos by Electra versus his characterization by the Messenger.

D. Comparisons Electra makes between her own ragged appearance and the appearance of her mother's finery, and even that of her mother's slaves.

E. The characterization of Orestes by Electra versus the character revealed by his own words and actions.

F. How these discrepancies reveal the state of Electra's mind, and suggest she is more concerned with the material things she's lost than with the loss of her father.

III. The Dangers of Relying on External Appearances

A. Orestes' monologue following his meeting with the Farmer.

B. The symbolic function of Orestes' scar, versus the other external signs of his identity.

C. The use of an image of Helen by Zeus to start the Trojan War, as related by Castor in the final episode.

IV. Euripides' purpose in playing the theme of appearance versus reality out throughout the play.

Topic #3

In Electra and Medea, Euripides has created unconventional female protagonists who are more self–willed than many others in Greek tragedy. Analyze the similarities and differences between the two.

Outline

I. Thesis Statement: *Euripides' Electra and Medea act in many ways that are contrary to what might be expected of traditional Greek women, but they are not cut from exactly the same cloth. In both their similarities and differences, they have been drawn unforgettably.*

II. Medea and Electra as Active rather than Passive Women

   A. How Medea takes matters in her own hands:

   1. Medea's history with Jason as related by both her and the Nurse.

   2. Medea's use of Aegeus, and his respect for her abilities to solve his problems.

   3. Medea's plans for revenge after her scene with Aegeus, and how she executes them.

   4. The Euripidean invention which made her famous.

   5. Her escape in the chariot of the sun god.

   B. Electra's Acts of Will

   1. Her declaration to arrange for her mother's murder, and her success in bringing her to the farmhouse.

   2. Her calls to Orestes' manhood when he is about to falter.

   3. Her role in the matricide.

III. Similarities

   A. Both are unwavering in their desire for revenge.

   B. Both defy the conventions of their societies, both in the acts of murder and in other ways. (Examples: Medea's outspokenness regarding women's roles; Electra's impiety in speaking over Aigisthos' body).

   C. Both are skilled in the arts of argumentation. (Examples: Medea's successful arguments with Creon, Jason, and Aegeus; Electra's successful arguments with Orestes and the Old Man).

   D. Both possess the will to carry out their actions, despite how "unnatural" they seem.

IV. Differences

    A. Medea only seems to care what others think about her, while Electra is constantly concerned about her appearance and jealous of her mother's.

    B. Medea is only hardened by her acts of murder, while Electra has a change of heart.

    C. Medea's actions are fueled by grand passions of love, while Electra's seem motivated more by pettier concerns of creature comfort and mother–envy.

    D. Medea has the foresight to plan for her safe escape; Electra hasn't seen past her act of revenge and loses almost everything she hoped to gain.

V. How Euripides was able to create realistic characters in both the similarities and differences between these two female protagonists.

Glossary of Greek and Latin Terms Used in this Study

Catharsis: purging or cleansing; in theatre through the experience of pity and fear.

Exodos: the final song and dance of the chorus as they exit the playing area.

Hamartia: literally, "missing the mark" (as in archery), usually translated as the "tragic flaw."

Hetairai: Greek courtesans.

Parados: the entrance of the chorus.

Peripeteia: a reversal or sudden change in fortune.

Polis: Greek city–state.

Stasima: choral songs.

Theologeion: literally, "stage of the gods," referring to a playing area on top of the structure forming the backdrop to the play's action, where the gods typically appear.

SECTION SIX

Bibliography

Quotations from *Medea* and *Electra* are taken from the following translations, and the numbers which follow them in parentheses refer to the page numbers in these texts:

Euripides. *Medea*. Tr. Alistair Elliot, with introduction by Nicholas Dromgoole. London: Oberon Books, 1993.

Euripides. *Electra*. Trs. Janet Lembke and Kenneth J. Reckford. New York and Oxford: Oxford University Press, 1994.

The introductions to both translations were invaluable to this study. In addition, the critical comments accompanying other translations were also consulted, as follows:

Euripides. *Medea*. Tr. Desmond Egan, Introduction by Brian Arkins. Laurinburg, NC: St. Andrews Press, 1991.

Euripides. *Medea*. Tr. Michael Townsend, Introduction by William Arrowsmith. Scranton, PA: Chandler Publishing Co., 1966.

Euripides. *The Medea of Euripides*. Tr. Rex Warner. New York: J. Chanticleer Press, 1944.

Euripides. *Electra*. Tr. Gilbert Murray. London: George Allen & Unwin Ltd., 1916.

Euripides. *Medea and Other Plays*. Tr. Philip Veracott. London: Penguin Books, 1963.

Euripides. *Electra*. Tr. Emily Townsend Vermeule. In *Euripides: The Complete Greek Tragedies*, vol. 5. David Grene and Richard Lattimore, eds. Chicago: University of Chicago Press, 1966.

The following sources were also valuable in providing critical and historical background:

Barlow, Shirley A. *The Imagery of Euripides*. Bristol: Bristol Classical Press, 1986.

Bates, William Nickerson. *Euripides: A Student of Human Nature*. Philadelphia: University of Pennsylvania Press, 1930.

Brockett, Oscar. *History of the Theatre*. Sixth Edition. Boston: Allyn and Bacon, 1991.

Conacher, D.J. *Euripides: Myth, Theme, and Structure*. Toronto: University of Toronto Press, 1967.

Decharme, Paul. *Euripides and the Spirit of His Dramas*. Tr. James Loeb. Port Washington, NY: Kennikat Press, 1968.

Greer, Thomas H. *A Brief History of Western Man*. Third Edition, New York: Harcourt Brace Jovanovich, 1977.

Jacobus, Lee A. *The Bedford Introduction to Drama*. New York: St. Martin's Press, 1989.

Laks, Batya Casper. *Electra: A Gender Sensitive Study of the Plays Based on the Myth*. Jefferson, NC and London: McFarland & Co., 1995.

Murray, Gilbert. *Euripides and His Age*. Cambridge, MA: Henry Holt and Co., 1913.

REA's **Problem Solvers**

The "PROBLEM SOLVERS" are comprehensive supplemental text-books designed to save time in finding solutions to problems. Each "PROBLEM SOLVER" is the first of its kind ever produced in its field. It is the product of a massive effort to illustrate almost any imaginable problem in exceptional depth, detail, and clarity. Each problem is worked out in detail with a step-by-step solution, and the problems are arranged in order of complexity from elementary to advanced. Each book is fully indexed for locating problems rapidly.

ACCOUNTING	HEAT TRANSFER
ADVANCED CALCULUS	LINEAR ALGEBRA
ALGEBRA & TRIGONOMETRY	MACHINE DESIGN
AUTOMATIC CONTROL	MATHEMATICS for ENGINEERS
SYSTEMS/ROBOTICS	MECHANICS
BIOLOGY	NUMERICAL ANALYSIS
BUSINESS, ACCOUNTING, & FINANCE	OPERATIONS RESEARCH
CALCULUS	OPTICS
CHEMISTRY	ORGANIC CHEMISTRY
COMPLEX VARIABLES	PHYSICAL CHEMISTRY
COMPUTER SCIENCE	PHYSICS
DIFFERENTIAL EQUATIONS	PRE-CALCULUS
ECONOMICS	PROBABILITY
ELECTRICAL MACHINES	PSYCHOLOGY
ELECTRIC CIRCUITS	STATISTICS
ELECTROMAGNETICS	STRENGTH OF MATERIALS &
ELECTRONIC COMMUNICATIONS	MECHANICS OF SOLIDS
ELECTRONICS	TECHNICAL DESIGN GRAPHICS
FINITE & DISCRETE MATH	THERMODYNAMICS
FLUID MECHANICS/DYNAMICS	TOPOLOGY
GENETICS	TRANSPORT PHENOMENA
GEOMETRY	VECTOR ANALYSIS

*If you would like more information about any of these books,
complete the coupon below and return it to us or visit your local bookstore.*